TOXIC MONEY, TAINTED MARRIAGES

Ignore money conversations long enough...
...and love starts to pay the price.

Amar Khanna

Clever Fox PUBLISHING

Chennai • Bangalore

CLEVER FOX PUBLISHING
Chennai, India

Published by CLEVER FOX PUBLISHING 2025

ISBN: 978-93-6707-748-1

Contents

Part 1: The Emotional Core of Money and Relationships 1

1. Introduction 2
2. Financial Compatibility vs. Chemistry 18
3. Income Imbalance and Power Dynamics 35

Part 2: Building a Financial Life Together 49

4. Joint Accounts vs. Separate Accounts 50
5. From Birth to School Fees 77
6. Emergency Funds and Financial Safety Nets: Preparing for the "What Ifs" as a Couple 95
7. Insurance: Love, and Liability 105
8. Retirement Planning as a Couple 129

Part 3: Outside Forces and High Stake Decisions 149

9. Family Pressure and Cultural Expectations 150
10. Financial Burnout and Emotional Toll 164

Part 1

The Emotional Core of Money and Relationships

Chapter 1

Introduction

Why Love and Money Don't Always Mix?

And Why It's Worth Fixing!

Let's be honest, talking about money with the person you love is *hard*. Sometimes, even harder than talking about your past, your fears, or your future dreams.

You can love someone deeply, laugh with them, build a life together, and still feel completely stuck, awkward, or even resentful when it comes to discussing money.

So, if you and your partner have ever:

- ❖ Argued over spending habits
- ❖ Felt nervous talking about income, debt, or savings
- ❖ Secretly judged each other's financial choices
- ❖ Avoided money talks altogether

You're not alone. And you're not broken. You're just human.

Why Is Couple Finance So Difficult?

It's because money is not just about money.

Money carries:

- Our childhood memories
- Our family values
- Our fears of failure
- Our dreams of security
- Our sense of control, freedom, and even self-worth

When two people come together, they don't just merge bank accounts; they merge belief systems, emotional baggage, spending patterns, and sometimes, totally opposite money personalities.

One might be a saver, the other a spender.

One might plan every rupee, the other might avoid budgeting altogether.

One might be carrying hidden debt, the other might be chasing financial freedom.

That's why love alone isn't enough to make a couple's finances work. You need tools, language, structure, and above all, mutual respect, and teamwork.

But Here's the Good News…

Money fights don't mean your relationship is doomed.

Financial stress doesn't mean you're incompatible.

And you don't need to be a finance expert to build a healthy money life together.

What you do need is the willingness to:

- Understand each other's financial mindset
- Talk openly without shame or blame
- Make joint decisions while honoring individual needs
- Create a system that feels fair—not 50/50, but 100/100 in effort and trust

Why I Wrote This Book

I've worked with hundreds of couples as a financial consultant. I've sat with partners who couldn't look each other in the eye when talking about money. I've witnessed tears, silence, anger, and I've also witnessed healing, laughter, and breakthroughs.

Every couple has their own money story.

This book is here to help you write yours, consciously, lovingly, and practically.

You'll learn:

- Why most couples avoid money talks
- How to deal with income imbalance, debt, and family pressure

- ❖ How to set up fair systems (even if one earns more or nothing at all)
- ❖ How to handle sensitive topics like spending habits, kids, and long-term goals
- ❖ And most importantly, how to turn money into a tool for connection, not conflict

This Book Is for You If…

- ❖ You're in a relationship and want to feel more financially aligned
- ❖ You keep avoiding money conversations, but know they're necessary
- ❖ You've had money fights and want a healthier way forward
- ❖ You want a step-by-step approach to managing money as a team

Whether you're dating, newly married, or decades into your relationship, this book will help you move from confusion to clarity, from conflict to cooperation.

A Quick Promise Before We Begin

This book won't lecture you. It's not about making you feel bad or telling you what's right or wrong.

It's here to offer insightful stories, simple frameworks, and real tools that work in the real world, with real emotions involved.

Because the goal isn't just financial stability, it's emotional safety around money.

Let's get started.

Your most honest, empowered money conversations begin here.

Part 1: The Emotional Core of Money and Relationships

1: Why Couples Struggle to Talk Openly About Money, And How to Fix It

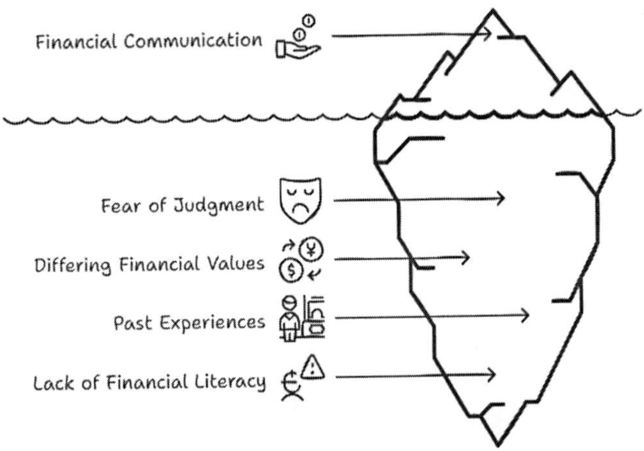

The Unspoken Taboo

In most relationships, money is the elephant in the room.

Couples talk about dreams, kids, careers, even in-laws, sometimes with passion, sometimes with frustration, but money?

That's often met with silence, evasion, or tension.

A 2022 survey by Fidelity found that 1 in 5 couples kept financial secrets from their partners, and more than 40% admitted to avoiding money conversations altogether.

These are not isolated incidents; they're part of a broader pattern of communication breakdowns around money.

Section 1:

The Roots of Financial Silence

Money isn't just about numbers. It's deeply emotional. It carries layers of meaning: safety, freedom, power, shame, success, and failure. What we believe about money is often shaped in childhood and reinforced by culture. And when two people come together in a relationship, they bring their unique financial histories, anxieties, and habits with them.

Some of the common psychological drivers behind financial avoidance in couples include:

- Fear of judgment: "If I tell them I'm in debt, they'll think I'm irresponsible."
- Shame: "I should have saved more by now."

- ❖ Power dynamics: "If I earn more, I'll have to control everything—or nothing."
- ❖ Avoidance as a coping strategy: "If we don't talk about it, maybe it'll go away."

Exploring the spectrum of emotional responses to financial discussions.

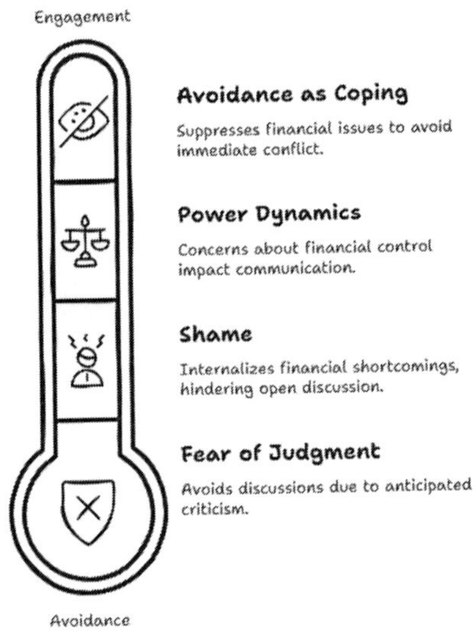

Let's understand the situation with an example (names changed)

Aarav and Neha had been married for four years. On the surface, everything seemed fine—they both had decent jobs, shared the rent, and went on vacations once a year. But behind the scenes, Neha was carrying a secret.

She had a credit card bill of ₹2.5 lakhs that Aarav didn't know about. It started with one impulsive purchase, then another. Over time, the guilt of hiding it became heavier than the debt itself. But she was afraid to tell him. She thought: "He'll never trust me again."

When Aarav eventually found out—through a bounced EMI from their joint account—the confrontation was explosive. Not because of the money, but because of the betrayal.

Their arguments weren't about ₹2.5 lakhs; they were about trust. Aarav felt deceived. Neha felt judged. The emotional wounds ran deeper than the financial ones.

Here is what we did –

Step 1: Immediate Financial Damage Control

- Open Full Disclosure
- Schedule a neutral, non-judgmental money talk session.
- Neha fully discloses her debt of ₹2.5 lakh and any other liabilities.
- Aarav discloses his financial status too.
- The rule is simple: no blaming, just stating facts.

List All Accounts and Debts.

Create a full list of credit cards, loans, bank accounts (individual and joint), incomes, and EMIs.

Create a Short-Term Action Plan

- Prioritize clearing the credit card debt, since it carries high interest.
- Explore options like debt consolidation loans, EMI restructuring, or a systematic payment plan.
- Decide together how much each partner can contribute monthly to clear the debt.

Step 2: Emotional Rebuilding – Re-establishing Financial Trust

Set a No Secrets Policy

Both partners agree that no new loans, credit cards, or large financial decisions will be made without informing each other.

Money Meetings

- Hold weekly 15-minute check-ins on finances.
- Track bills, savings, and debt repayment progress.
- Celebrate small milestones to stay motivated, for example paying off ₹50,000 of debt.

Financial Transparency Tools

Use a shared spreadsheet or financial app like Splitwise, Mint, or a simple Excel sheet to track expenses.

Step 3: Building a Joint Financial Vision

Shared Financial Goals

Work together to define and agree on common goals such as:

- Building an emergency fund of six months of expenses
- Saving for annual vacations
- Investing for retirement

Budget Planning

Create a realistic monthly budget that covers necessities, debt repayment, savings, and personal spending.

The aim is to balance discipline with enough flexibility to avoid resentment.

Allow Individual Freedom

Assign each partner a small personal monthly allowance, for example, ₹5,000 each, to spend without any explanation.

This reduces the temptation to hide spending.

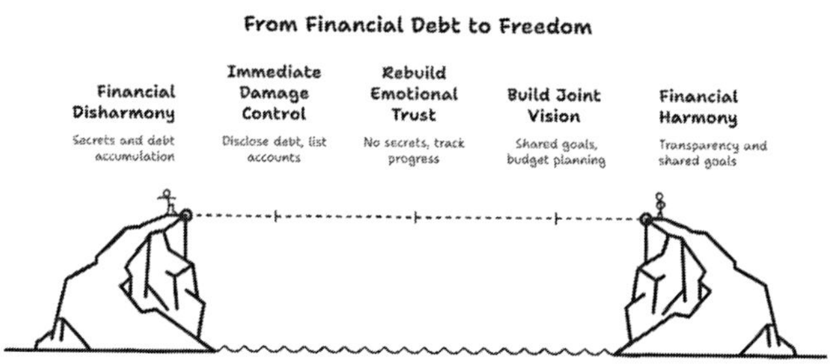

Case Study 2

Kavya and Rahul had just moved in together. Rahul worked in tech and earned significantly more than Kavya, who was building her photography business. At first, Kavya was hesitant to bring up money—she feared being seen as "less successful." Meanwhile, Rahul didn't want to "make her feel bad," so he avoided discussing his income.

They consulted me regarding the issue. Here is what I suggested:

Step 1: Creating a Safe Space for Money Conversations

- I advised Kavya and Rahul to schedule a dedicated time for an open financial discussion.
- The goal was to focus not just on numbers but also on emotions, insecurities, and expectations related to money.
- They were encouraged to approach the conversation with honesty and without judgment.
- Each partner shared their financial realities, including income, expenses, debts, and emotional concerns around money.

Step 2: Acknowledging Emotional Differences

- We worked through the feelings behind the money.
- Kavya expressed her fear of appearing dependent. Rahul shared his concern about being resented for earning more.

- Understanding that money conversations are emotional, not just practical, helped them lower defensiveness and build empathy toward each other.

Step 3: Setting Up a Proportional Contribution System

- Instead of splitting shared expenses 50-50, I suggested a proportional system based on income.
- Each partner would contribute a fair percentage of their income toward joint expenses like rent, groceries, utilities, and vacations.
- This system allowed both to feel like equal partners, without one feeling burdened or the other feeling guilty.

Step 4: Establishing Regular Financial Check-Ins

We agreed that financial conversations should not be one-time events.

Kavya and Rahul committed to meeting every three months for a financial review.

In these meetings, they would assess:

- ❖ Changes in income
- ❖ Adjustments needed in contributions
- ❖ Upcoming financial goals
- ❖ Any emotional challenges or shifts

The rule was clear: no blame, only reflection and adjustment.

Step 5: Building Joint and Individual Financial Goals

- Along with shared expenses, I helped them outline personal and joint goals.
- Joint goals included building an emergency fund, saving for travel, and investing for the future.
- Individual goals respected their separate ambitions, like Kavya growing her photography business and Rahul saving for advanced tech courses.

In Summary

- ❖ Create a safe space for financial discussions
- ❖ Acknowledge the emotional aspects of money
- ❖ Use proportional contribution instead of 50-50
- ❖ Schedule quarterly money check-ins
- ❖ Set joint and individual financial goals

Conclusion-

Money Talk = Love Talk

Why are conversations about money the most intimate and transformative talks a couple can have?

When we think about intimacy, we often think of deep conversations, shared experiences, and emotional vulnerability. But there's one area that quietly holds all of these and more: money.

Talking openly about money isn't just about numbers on a spreadsheet; it's about values, security, dreams, fears, and respect. It's where love meets logistics, and where our personal histories collide with our shared future.

And yet… many couples avoid it.

Why?

Because money talk is vulnerable. It exposes how we were raised, what we fear, what we want, and what we feel we deserve. It can trigger shame, defensiveness, or even conflict. But here's the truth: the silence is far more dangerous than the discomfort.

Silence breeds distance.

When couples don't talk about money, they don't just avoid budgetingthey avoid each other. They stay silent about goals, about debt, about the anxiety of financial uncertainty. That silence can slowly build walls, walls that create misunderstanding, resentment, or mistrust.

You might think, "We just have different money styles," or "It's easier not to bring it up." But every unspoken worry or assumption becomes a weight the relationship quietly carries.

Honesty builds connections.

The act of sitting down and saying, "Here's what I earn. Here's what I owe. Here's what I dream about," is incredibly intimate. It's raw. It's real. And it tells your partner: I trust you with who I am.

You don't have to agree on every line item. One of you might be a spender, the other a saver. One might crave security, the other dreams of adventure. The goal isn't perfect alignment, it's shared understanding.

When couples talk openly about money:

- They align on goals (even if they approach them differently)
- They plan for emergencies and dreams alike
- They create a sense of team, not tension
- They reduce conflict by increasing clarity

Money stops being a power struggle and starts being a tool, one that supports both partners' visions for life.

Conversations to have

- How do we make decisions, jointly or individually?
- What's our approach to saving, spending, and giving?
- How do we handle debt?
- What's our plan for big milestones, kids, homes, retirement?
- What emotions do we each attach to money?

Each of these talks builds trust. Not just financial trust, but emotional trust.

Because when couples learn to talk about money, they're not just managing their finances.

They're strengthening their bond.

They're saying, I see you. I hear you. I want to build this life with you.

Your next step: Start small. Ask your partner,

"What did money feel like growing up?"

Let that one question open the door. Be curious, not critical. Listen more than you speak.

The goal isn't to fix, it's to connect.

Because money talk?

Is love talk.

Chapter 2

Financial Compatibility vs. Chemistry

What Happens When a Spender Marries a Saver—Or Worse

The Sweet Spot for Lasting Relationships

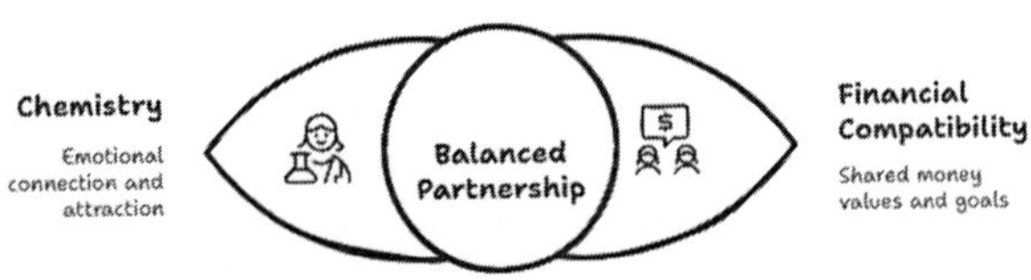

Love Isn't Always Enough!

Romantic chemistry can sweep people off their feet. But when the honeymoon phase fades and everyday financial decisions kick in, money habits start to matter—a lot.

What seemed like charming quirks ("She's so spontaneous!" or "He's super organized!") can quickly become flashpoints for conflict. Financial compatibility isn't about having the same income level—it's about how two people think, feel, and behave around money.

And when those styles differ significantly, couples can find themselves locked in recurring arguments over budgets, savings, lifestyle, and values.

The 5 Common Money Personalities

Every person has a "money personality," a set of attitudes and behaviors shaped by upbringing, culture, personal experiences, and emotional associations with money. Here are five common ones:

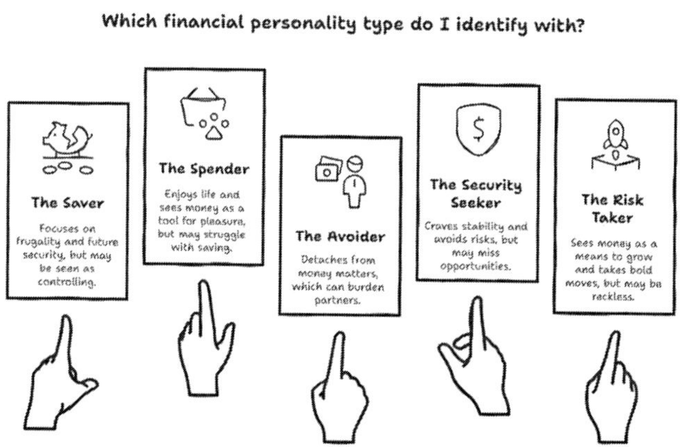

1. The Saver

- Focuses on frugality, future security, and financial discipline.
- Finds comfort in budgeting, hates debt, and is proud of not being "wasteful."
- Strengths: Long-term planning, resilience in emergencies.
- Challenges: Can come off as controlling, stingy, or joyless to others.

2. The Spender

- Loves to enjoy life and sees money as a tool for pleasure, experiences, or status.
- Often makes impulsive purchases and may struggle with long-term saving.
- Strengths: Generous, optimistic, and often a joy to be around.
- Challenges: May avoid budgeting or feel anxious when restricted.

3. The Avoider

- Detaches from money matters out of fear, anxiety, or lack of interest.
- Often ignores bills, avoids planning, or delegates finances to their partner.
- Strengths: Flexible and low-maintenance.

- Challenges: Can leave the partner feeling overburdened or insecure.

4. **The Security Seeker**

- Craves stability, risk aversion, and predictability.
- Invests cautiously, prefers insurance, and safe bets.
- Strengths: Great at contingency planning.
- Challenges: May resist opportunities or be overly anxious about "what-ifs."

5. **The Risk Taker**

- Sees money as a means to grow, explore, and take bold moves.
- Loves investing, entrepreneurial ventures, or crypto.
- Strengths: Visionary, confident, future-focused.
- Challenges: Can be reckless or leave partners in the dark about risks.

PERSONALITY ASSESSMENT QUIZ

Money Personality Assessment: What's Your Financial Style?

1. When you receive a surprise bonus, your first instinct is to...
   A) Put it straight into savings.
   B) Treat yourself, you earned it!
   C) Forget about it until someone reminds you.

D) Move it into a safe investment or emergency fund.

E) Use it to invest in something with growth potential.

2. How do you feel about budgeting?

A) I love it, it gives me peace of mind.

B) I find it restrictive and boring.

C) I usually avoid it until it's urgent.

D) I follow one religiously.

E) I don't mind if it allows me to take financial risks strategically.

3. When a friend suggests an expensive vacation, you...

A) Decline and suggest something cheaper.

B) Say yes, life's too short to say no.

C) Say "maybe" and never really follow up.

D) Run a cost-benefit analysis before making a decision.

E) Think, "Can I turn this into a networking or business opportunity?"

4. Your biggest financial fear is...

A) Not having enough in an emergency.

B) Missing out on life experiences.

C) Having to face my finances alone.

D) Losing control over my money.

E) Not growing my wealth fast enough.

5. How often do you check your bank or investment accounts?
   A) Every few days—I keep close tabs.
   B) Only when I have to.
   C) Rarely—I try not to look.
   D) Weekly, with a spreadsheet.
   E) Frequently—I'm watching the markets or my business closely.

6. Your view on credit cards is...
   A) Dangerous if not managed carefully.
   B) Helpful for enjoying life now.
   C) Complicated—I just pay the minimum and move on.
   D) Useful for building credit, but must be tracked.
   E) A strategic tool to fund opportunities.

7. Your idea of a perfect financial future is...
   A) A well-stocked retirement fund and zero debt.
   B) A life full of travel, freedom, and comfort.
   C) One where I don't have to think about money.
   D) A stable, predictable income with strong insurance.
   E) High earnings, bold investments, and financial independence early.

8. In a relationship, financial decisions should be...
   A) Cautious and jointly agreed upon
   B) Flexible so both people can enjoy their lives.
   C) Handled by the more financially savvy person.
   D) Carefully planned and written down. E) Made with long-term strategy and upside in mind.

9. You receive a big bill unexpectedly. You:
   A) Pull from your emergency fund without panic.
   B) Feel annoyed that it ruins your plans, but figure it out.
   C) Ignore it for now, it's overwhelming.
   D) Adjust your budget and cover it immediately.
   E) Consider using debt creatively or restructuring to absorb it.

10. How do you typically approach investing?
    A) Conservatively, low risk, steady growth.
    B) I rarely invest; I prefer spending in the now.
    C) I haven't started, it feels intimidating.
    D) I research safe options before committing.
    E) I go after high-growth opportunities, even if risky.

11. When talking about money with your partner, you usually...
    A) Focus on saving goals and responsible choices.
    B) Talk about lifestyle goals and fun things.
    C) Avoid the conversation if possible.

   D) Stick to the facts and plans.
   E) Pitch ideas and opportunities.

12. What was your money lesson growing up?
   A) "Save for a rainy day."
   B) "Money is meant to be enjoyed."
   C) "We didn't talk about money much."
   D) "Be prepared for anything."
   E) "Take risks if you want to get ahead."

13. How do you handle financial setbacks?
   A) Cut expenses and adjust.
   B) Stress, but I try to carry on.
   C) Hope they go away.
   D) Re-strategize carefully.
   E) Double down and find a new opportunity.

14. Your ideal money app would...
   A) Help me track and save more efficiently.
   B) Make spending and lifestyle planning easy.
   C) Require minimal interaction.
   D) Show projections and risk analysis.
   E) Recommend aggressive investment ideas.

15. How do you define financial success?
   A) Security and peace of mind.
   B) Freedom to do what I want.
   C) Not having to worry or think about money.
   D) Being in full control of my finances.
   E) Building wealth and leaving a legacy.

Scoring Guide:

Mostly A = Saver

Mostly B = Spender

Mostly C = Avoider

Mostly D = Security Seeker

Mostly E = Risk Taker

UNDERSTANDING THE CONFLICTS -

Saver vs. Spender: The Tug of War Between Control and Freedom

In this dynamic, the Saver constantly feels like they're the only one holding the financial line, tightening the budget, tracking expenses, and worrying about tomorrow. The Spender, meanwhile, feels boxed in, like life is passing them by while they're stuck counting pennies.

The Saver may interpret the Spender's choices as careless or even selfish, while the Spender sees the Saver as rigid, joyless, or controlling.

Over time, the Saver starts to resent being the "parent" in the relationship, while the Spender feels like a child being policed. Beneath the surface is often a much deeper fear: for the Saver, it's fear of instability; for the Spender, it's fear of missing out on life itself. These conflicting fears can only be reconciled through shared values, not just spreadsheets.

Avoider vs. Security Seeker: The Silent Storm

This couple often looks calm on the outside, but under the surface, tension builds.

The Security Seeker lives for financial clarity. They crave plans, spreadsheets, and certainty. Meanwhile, the Avoider runs from the very thing their partner leans on. Money conversations make them anxious or bored.

They'd rather not open the bank app, and if left alone, they might ignore bills or make last-minute financial decisions. For the Security Seeker, this creates chronic stress—they feel they can't rely on their partner or fully relax. For the Avoider, constant nudging feels like pressure, criticism, or even shame. What starts as a personality difference quickly becomes an emotional wedge. The real work here is in building safety around financial conversations, so the Avoider doesn't shut down and the Security Seeker doesn't burn out trying to control everything.

Risk Taker vs. Saver: The Visionary and the Vault

This pairing can feel electric or explosive. The Risk Taker sees opportunity everywhere: startups, crypto, business ventures. They believe in bold moves and are often driven by excitement, confidence, and a belief that "you have to spend money to make money." The Saver, by contrast, finds comfort in predictability.

They want to protect what's already been earned, not gamble it. To the Saver, the Risk Taker is reckless; to the Risk Taker, the Saver is a dream-killer. What's really happening is a deeper battle between future visions, one is imagining safety, the other, success. Trust becomes fragile in this pairing if there isn't transparency.

The key is co-creating a financial plan that respects both security and growth a "safe-to-risk" fund, for instance, can help both feel seen and respected.

Case studies –

Raj and Meera – The Saver and the Spender

Raj and Meera aren't just arguing about money; they're reacting from deeply rooted money beliefs shaped by their upbringing.

Raj's identity is tied to responsibility and security; saving gives him control in a world that feels uncertain.

Meera's approach is built on joy, generosity, and the belief that money is meant to be enjoyed while you can. Their arguments aren't just about expenses, they're about values. And because they didn't know how to bridge those values, they started hiding things from each other, purchases, emotions, and over time, trust.

The real problem isn't the spending, it's the structure.

How to balance financial values in a relationship?

Raj
Security and Control

Meera
Joy and Generosity

Here's what I often see: couples like Raj and Meera aren't financially incompatible; they just lack a shared money system that respects both personalities.

Let's walk through a solution.

1. Create a "Yours, Mine & Ours" Budget System
   Instead of using one joint account for everything, Raj and Meera can use a hybrid model:
   - Joint account ("Ours"): For shared essentials like rent, groceries, utilities, and savings goals
   - Individual accounts ("Yours" and "Mine"): Each partner gets a monthly discretionary allowance, no questions asked

This gives Raj structure and predictability, while Meera gains freedom and autonomy. No more guilt for treating herself. No more surprise expenses that make Raj panic.

2. Set a Monthly "Money Ritual"
   Instead of reacting in the heat of the moment, they can schedule a money date once a month, a glass of wine, phones away, open up the budget and talk. Not just about numbers, but about how money is feeling that month.
   Is Raj feeling anxious about savings? Is Meera feeling stifled? This ritual turns conflict into connection.

3. Define Shared Values and Make Them Tangible
   Raj and Meera should create a short list of shared money goals:
   - A yearly travel fund (Meera's joy)
   - An emergency fund target (Raj's peace of mind)
   - A "fun fund" for spontaneous outings or gifts

When both partners see their priorities reflected in the financial plan, the tension eases.

4. Use Language That Builds Trust
   Raj should swap criticism ("Did we need to go out?") for curiosity ("What did you love about that night?"). Meera should swap defensiveness ("We're not broke!") for empathy ("I know you get stressed when we spend more than usual, can we talk about what's okay for this month?"). Money is emotional, and language either escalates or soothes.

Case Study-2

Aisha and Dev – The Avoider and the Security Seeker

Aisha, a freelance graphic designer, is spontaneous and creative, not just in her work, but in how she lives. Her relationship with money is simple: she avoids it. Bills stress her out. Budgets feel like cages.

She'd rather focus on the now and trust things will "somehow work out."

Dev, her partner, is a high school teacher raised in a home where security was everything. His father was laid off twice, and his mother made sure every rupee was accounted for. Now, as an adult, Dev finds comfort in monthly spreadsheets, financial checklists, and long-term plans. He needs predictability. Aisha needs space.

The conflict started small: Dev would ask about shared expenses or the rent, and Aisha would say, "I'll figure it out this week." Weeks passed. Payments were late. Dev began to panic. He felt like he was carrying the mental load alone. Aisha, on the other hand, felt judged and overwhelmed, like she was being audited by her own partner.

Eventually, Dev started checking Aisha's accounts behind her back. Aisha found out. And just like that, the issue wasn't about money anymore; it was about trust, privacy, and respect.

The Core Issue: Emotional Safety Looks Different to Each of Them

Dev seeks financial safety through control. Aisha seeks emotional safety through freedom. They're not wrong, just unaligned.

I've seen this dynamic many times. The Security Seeker needs clarity. The Avoider needs a non-intimidating way to stay engaged. The key isn't to force one partner into the other's world—it's to create a middle ground where both feel safe enough to participate.

Here's what I recommend.

1. Use a Visual, Low-Tech Budgeting Tool
   Traditional spreadsheets overwhelm Aisha. Instead, they can use a color-coded wall calendar or whiteboard with simple categories: bills, savings goals, fun spending. It should live in a shared space like the kitchen, not buried in an app or file. Aisha doesn't need to manage the system, but she does need to see it regularly.

2. Switch from Monthly Reviews to Weekly Check-Ins
   Dev feels most secure with regular check-ins. But for Aisha, monthly budget meetings are too dense and

intimidating. Instead, they agree to 10-minute weekly "money huddles" every Sunday—short, casual, and consistent. This lowers the emotional temperature for both.

3. Automate Everything Possible
   To reduce stress on both sides, automate bill payments, savings transfers, and even reminders for shared financial goals. Automation takes the pressure off Aisha to "remember" and off Dev to "nag."

4. Assign Roles Based on Strengths, Not Fairness
   Instead of splitting financial tasks 50/50, divide responsibilities based on comfort and competence. Dev can manage the tracking and planning. Aisha can focus on creative goal-setting, like planning their anniversary trip within a budget. This way, both contribute without being forced into uncomfortable roles.

5. Create a "No Judgment" Space Around Mistakes
   When avoiders feel shamed, they shut down. Dev must learn to approach slip-ups with curiosity, not criticism. Aisha, in turn, must learn to stay in the room, even when it's hard. Building a financial partnership means both partners stretch a little, but never to the point of breaking.

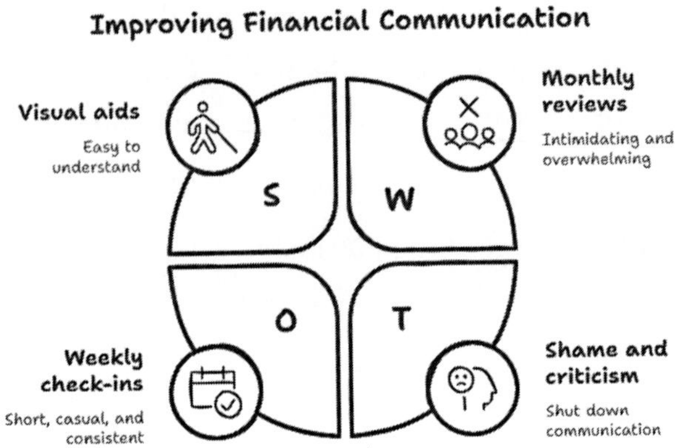
Improving Financial Communication
Visual aids
Easy to understand
S
Monthly reviews
Intimidating and overwhelming
W
O
Weekly check-ins
Short, casual, and consistent
T
Shame and criticism
Shut down communication

Chapter 3

Income Imbalance and Power Dynamics

Money, Resentment, and Modern Breadwinning

Income inequality causes unequal access and affects stability.

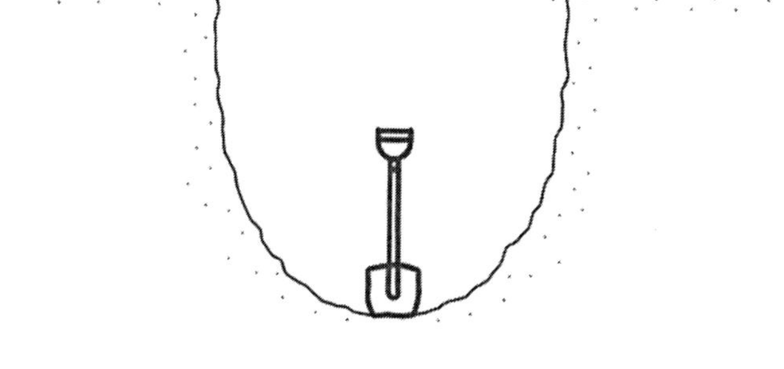

Introduction

In every couple, money flows differently, but when that flow becomes unequal, it often creates invisible tension. Income imbalance is one of the most common, least discussed, and deeply emotional dynamics in relationships. It doesn't just influence how much money goes into a joint account; it influences decision-making, self-worth, power, and how love is expressed and experienced.

This chapter explores what income imbalance does to couples, not just financially, but relationally and psychologically, and how to consciously manage the dynamics it creates.

Understanding Income Imbalance

Income imbalance refers to a situation where one partner earns significantly more than the other. This difference may result from career choices, life stages, caregiving responsibilities, health conditions, or personal priorities. The disparity itself is not inherently problematic; it becomes an issue when it creates imbalance in power, autonomy, and emotional connection.

In many cultures, especially those where gender roles are traditionally defined, income is tied to status and control. As society transitions into more equitable but still evolving structures, couples often find themselves caught between inherited roles and modern expectations.

Core Challenges Created by Income Imbalance

1. Power and Decision-Making

   When one partner contributes more financially, they may unconsciously (or consciously) feel entitled to make bigger decisions, from daily spending to long-term goals. This can create a subtle or overt power differential where the lower-earning partner's voice is minimized.

   Power should be shared, regardless of income, but income imbalance often challenges this principle.

2. Guilt and Resentment

   - The higher-earning partner may feel pressure to "carry the weight" and resentment if their efforts feel underappreciated.
   - The lower-earning partner may feel guilt over not contributing "enough," even if they add value in other non-financial ways like caregiving, emotional support, or household management.

These emotions, if unacknowledged, build quiet walls between partners.

3. Reduced Financial Autonomy

   When one partner earns significantly less (or nothing), they may feel they need "permission" to spend money, even for personal needs. This leads to decreased confidence and increased dependency, undermining the principle of partnership.

4. Lifestyle Mismatch
   Disparities in income can result in differences in lifestyle expectations. One partner may afford luxuries that the other feels uncomfortable with. If this isn't discussed openly, it can create pressure, embarrassment, or avoidance around shared experiences.

5. Distorted Equality
   Income imbalance often gets mistaken for inequality in value. The person bringing in more money may not acknowledge the unseen labor, whether it's managing the home, parenting, or emotional labor, that the other partner contributes.

True equality in a relationship is not based on equal income, but on mutual respect and fairness.

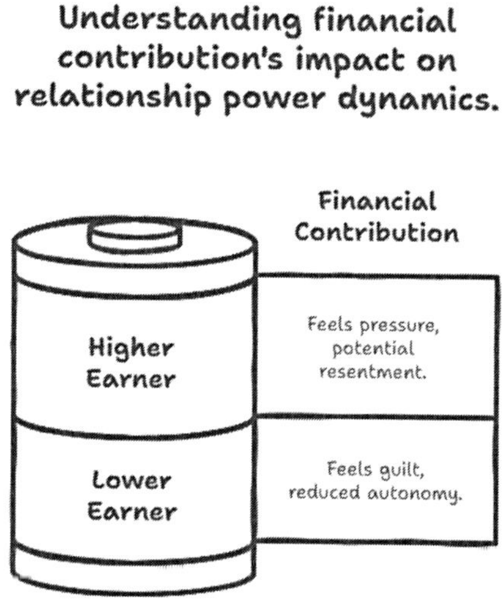

The Cultural Overlay -

In many societies, including India, the concept of the "breadwinner" is deeply gendered and hierarchical. Men are expected to provide; women are expected to support. These assumptions are changing, but slowly. When women out-earn men, it can trigger feelings of inadequacy. When men don't earn, they may feel displaced from traditional roles.

Modern couples must actively deconstruct these inherited beliefs and redefine success, partnership, and contribution on their own terms.

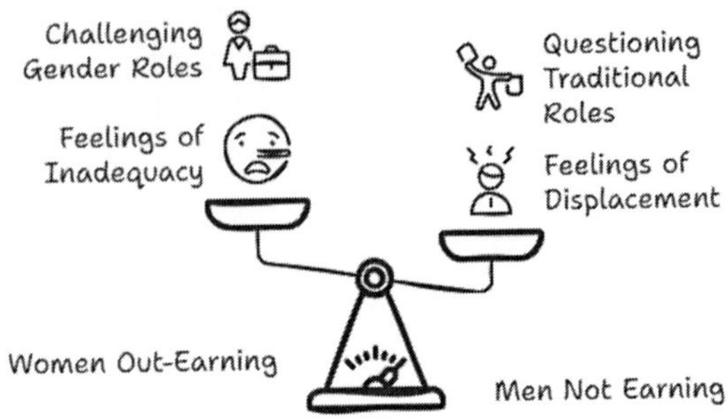

Balancing Emotional and Societal Shifts in Modern Partnerships

Financial Equity vs. Financial Equality

A common mistake couples make is to aim for "equality" in financial contributions, splitting bills 50/50, even when incomes differ drastically. This leads to strain on the lower earner and power imbalances in decision-making.

Instead, couples should aim for financial equity, a system that acknowledges the difference in income and distributes responsibilities in a fair, values-aligned way.

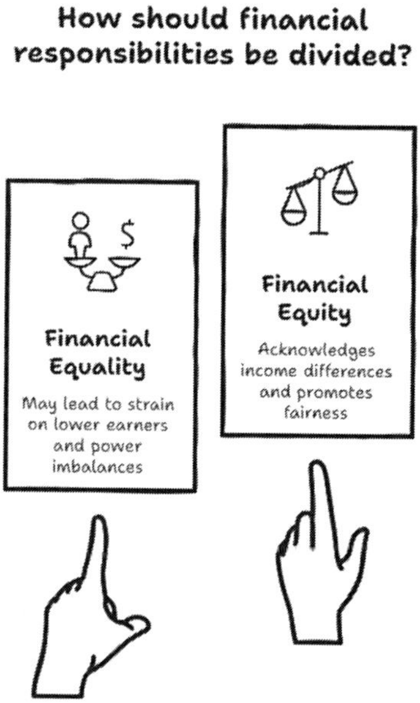

Case Study 1: Arjun and Omar

Two Cultures, One Closet, and the Cost of Silence

The Story

Arjun, originally from Mumbai, had lived in Dubai for eight years, climbing the corporate ladder in an international logistics firm. He earned a high six-figure AED salary and lived a carefully curated life, professionally successful, socially discreet.

Omar, his partner of four years, was a Syrian expat and self-employed interior designer with an inconsistent income. Omar was warm, artistic, and emotionally expressive, but had always felt financially insecure, not just because of his earnings, but because of the cultural and legal context they lived in.

Being in a gay relationship in a country like the UAE meant their relationship existed in a bubble, deeply intimate but entirely hidden. They shared a rented villa, expenses, vacations, and even a pet, but not a bank account. Not even a clear conversation about money.

Arjun paid for most things silently, believing that "love means not making him feel small." Omar, though grateful, grew uncomfortable. His occasional efforts to contribute were waved off. Slowly, admiration turned into resentment.

They began fighting about unrelated things—plans, attention, time. Money wasn't the topic. But it was always under the surface.

How I Helped Them, Step-by-Step

Step 1: Invite the Unspoken into the Room

Our first session was quiet, tense. When I asked about money, Omar said, "I just want to feel I'm not a kept secret and a kept man."

That sentence cracked the silence.

Arjun admitted he felt responsible, but also guilty—he assumed paying for everything showed love. Omar didn't want to be taken care of. He wanted to be seen as an equal.

Step 2: Honor Cultural and Emotional Complexities

This wasn't just a budgeting issue. It was about identity, freedom, and safety.

We talked about how their relationship operated in the shadows, emotionally and financially. Money had become another thing they couldn't openly share, even with each other.

They cried. Then they laughed. Then they talked. For the first time in a long time.

Step 3: Design a Discreet but Equal System

We created a digital structure that protected their privacy while offering shared visibility:

A shared virtual budget planner (no joint accounts needed)

A contribution tracker based on percentage, not amount

A goal planner with mutual rewards, like upgrading Omar's design software or planning a Europe trip.

Arjun no longer carried the burden alone. Omar no longer felt invisible.

Step 4: Monthly "Check-In Walks"

Since open conversations were hard at home, we created a ritual, monthly money walks on Jumeirah beach. One partner talks, the other listens. No fixing. Just presence.

That became their safe space. Money now flowed with meaning, not guilt.

Case Study 2: Isha and Rohan

Two Countries, One Future, and a Silent Rift

The Story

Isha, a UX designer from Pune, had taken a two-year assignment in Berlin with a leading fintech startup. Rohan, her partner of four years, was based in Singapore, working as a senior developer on contract with a global tech firm.

Their relationship had grown in India, shared coffee dates, spontaneous drives, and long phone calls through busy workdays. But ever since they moved abroad for their careers, a quiet shift began. Time zones, currencies, and emotional bandwidth had all changed.

The love was still there. But something was off.

Their conversations were now more transactional than tender:

"Did you manage to pay the LIC premium?"

"I sent money to your parents for the flat maintenance."

"What's the exchange rate this month?"

Isha earned in euros, Rohan in Singapore dollars. Their financial lives had become separate streams, flowing in different directions. Yet, the real tension wasn't about money; it was about unspoken expectations.

When Rohan booked a fancy resort for a reunion trip without asking, Isha felt overwhelmed and left out. When Isha asked if they could split travel expenses more evenly, Rohan was surprised—and a little hurt.

Then came the breaking point.

"I feel like I'm just managing the relationship," Isha said one evening.

"And I feel like I'm funding it," Rohan replied.

How I Helped Them, Step-by-Step

Step 1: Acknowledge the Emotional

Cost of Distance

Instead of diving into numbers, I asked, “What part of this relationship feels heavy?”

That question opened a door.

Isha admitted feeling like the emotional and logistical manager, always adjusting her schedule, booking flights, and keeping in touch with both families. Rohan confessed that while he earned more, he often felt disconnected, like he was expected to contribute money but not emotionally.

They weren’t fighting about money.

They were fighting about feeling unbalanced and unseen.

Step 2: Make the Invisible Visible

We mapped their real (not assumed) contributions:

Isha: Relationship planning, travel logistics, family coordination, emotional labor

Rohan: Rent for their home in Pune, investment management, emergency fund building

This reframing helped both realize:

They weren’t unequal, they were just uncoordinated.

Step 3: Flexible Contribution Ratio

We created a new approach:

Rohan would handle 60% of their joint financial goals, given his higher income

Isha would take the lead on travel and care logistics

Each would maintain personal accounts for autonomy

The result? No more resentment, no more second-guessing contributions.

Step 4: A Shared "Life Dashboard"

We set up a Google Sheet and Notion board where they:

Tracked savings (for a wedding, relocation, and home down payment)

Updated each other monthly on personal spending goals

Logged tasks and responsibilities, so invisible labor became visible and valued

Now, money wasn't a surprise topic; it was a shared project.

Step 5: Monthly "Mirror Calls"

Every first Sunday, they now have a video call where they answer:

"Where did we support each other well this month?"

"Where do we need more balance?"

"What money decision made you feel good or bad?"

These calls brought their emotional and financial lives back into sync.

Strategies for Healthy Financial Dynamics

Characteristic	Description
Shared Vision	Discuss goals together, allow individual contributions
Transparent Budgeting	Collaborative plan for expenses, needs, savings
Autonomy	Personal funds for independence, dignity, freedom
Proportional Contribution	Contribute percentage of income for fairness
Non-Monetary Contributions	Acknowledge emotional labor, household work value
Regular Check-Ins	Review budgets, goals, emotional temperature

Part 2

Building a Financial Life Together

Chapter 4

Joint Accounts vs. Separate Accounts

How to Structure Your Finances as a Team

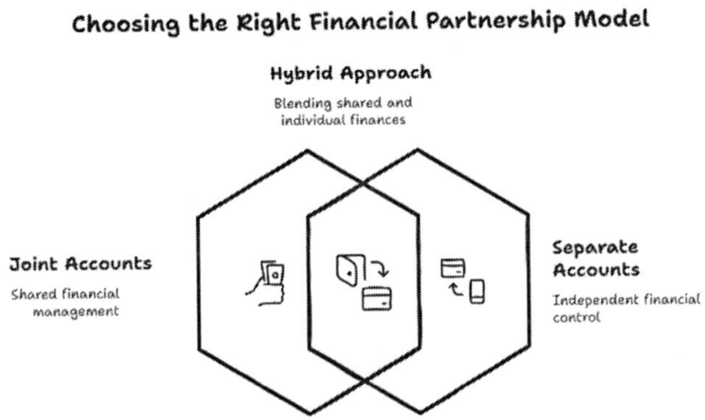

"Should we merge all our money or keep it separate?"

This is one of the most common questions I hear from couples right after "Should we talk about money at all?"

The truth is, there's no perfect formula. Every couple is different. But your money structure should do one important thing:

Support your relationship, not strain it.

Let's break this down simply.

This chapter will help you understand how to structure your bank accounts, depending on your situation and personality as a couple.

Why Your Money Structure Matters

How you manage money as a couple affects:

- ❖ Your trust in each other
- ❖ Your sense of independence and security
- ❖ How often do you argue (or avoid) money conversations
- ❖ Your ability to plan for the future together

A messy or unclear money system often leads to resentment, power imbalance, or financial insecurity.

The 3 Most Common Ways Couples Manage Money

Let's start with the basics.

Way-1

Fully Joint Accounts

A model based on complete sharing and complete trust

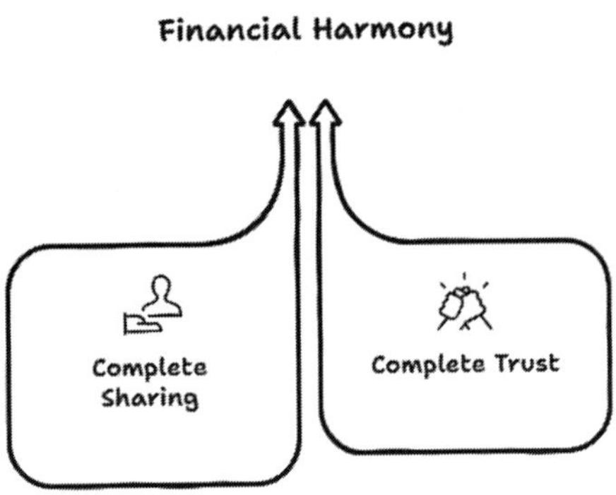

The fully joint account system is the traditional way many couples have managed their finances, especially in earlier generations. It operates on a simple premise:

"What's mine is yours, and what's yours is mine."

In this model, both partners pool all of their income into a single, shared account, and all household expenses, bills, groceries, rent, EMIs, vacations, investments, are paid from that same account. There are no personal or individual accounts. Everything flows through one stream.

While this method may seem old-fashioned to some, it can be deeply effective and emotionally fulfilling for couples who are completely financially aligned.

Who is this ideal for?

- Couples who have very high levels of trust and open communication
- Partnerships where both people are comfortable with full transparency
- Relationships where financial power isn't misused or unevenly distributed
- Often, couples who have been together for a long time or have a more traditional view of marriage

It's also commonly used by:

- Couples who have similar spending habits
- Households with one primary earner and one non-earning partner (e.g., stay-at-home spouse)
- Couples in early-stage marriages who are trying to build a unified life from the start

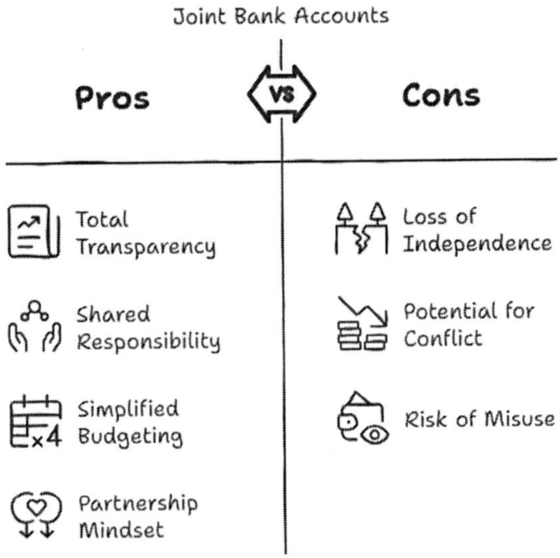

Benefits of Fully Joint Accounts

1. Total Transparency
   You always know where the money is coming from and where it's going. There's little room for financial secrecy.
2. Shared Ownership and Responsibility
   This model reinforces the idea that both partners are building a life *together*. Whether one earns more or less, both feel like equal contributors to the household.
3. Simplified Budgeting and Expense Tracking
   It's easier to manage monthly expenses, track spending patterns, and plan long-term goals when all transactions are visible in one account.

4. Encourages Partnership Mindset
   Psychologically, pooling finances can increase emotional bonding and reduce the "mine vs. yours" dynamic. You stop thinking like two individuals and start functioning as one financial team.

Risks and Challenges

Of course, this model isn't for everyone. It comes with a few caution points:

1. Loss of Autonomy
   Some individuals feel like they've lost control over their money, especially if their partner questions every purchase or spending decision. Even minor expenses may begin to feel "monitored."
2. Potential Power Imbalance
   If one partner earns significantly more and still wants to control the way money is spent, this setup can create tension and resentment. It can feel like one person is funding the relationship while the other is dependent, even if the non-earning partner contributes in invisible ways.

3. Risk of Misuse
   In cases where trust is shaky or communication is weak, joint accounts can make people feel vulnerable. If one partner has impulsive spending habits or isn't financially responsible, the other may feel exposed or unsafe.

4. Blurred Boundaries

   Without clear personal boundaries, disagreements can arise about individual purchases, hobbies, gifts, or family responsibilities (e.g., sending money to one's parents).

How to Make Fully Joint Accounts Work Smoothly

If this model speaks to you, here's how to set it up successfully:

1. Establish Ground Rules Early

   Have a detailed conversation around:

   - Monthly budget
   - Personal spending limits
   - Handling family support (on both sides)
   - Emergency expenses

2. Treat All Income as Equal

   Regardless of who earns more, consider the income *joint property*. One person may bring money, the other may contribute in time, care, or managing the home. Both deserve equal respect.

3. Agree on Spending Limits

   Some couples set a rule like:

   "Any purchase above ₹5,000 must be discussed together," even if there's enough money in the bank.

4. Schedule Monthly Money Meetings

Talk openly about expenses, upcoming needs, and emotional stress around finances. Treat it like a team check-in, not an audit.

5. Don't Forget Personal Freedom
   Even with one account, consider budgeting monthly personal allowance amounts for each partner. That way, you can enjoy autonomy without secrecy.

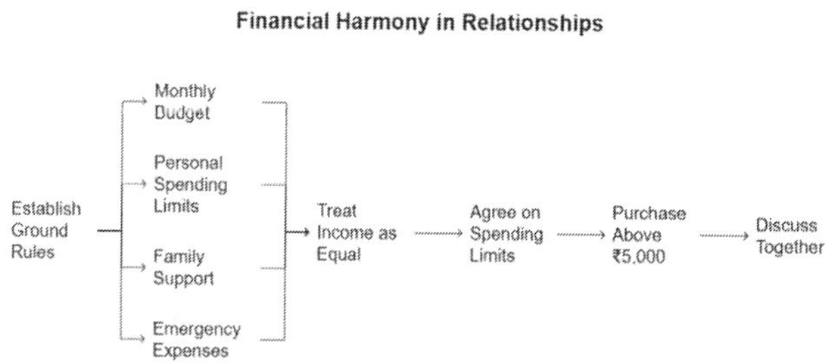

Way-2

Fully Separate Accounts

Independence and Clear Boundaries in Love

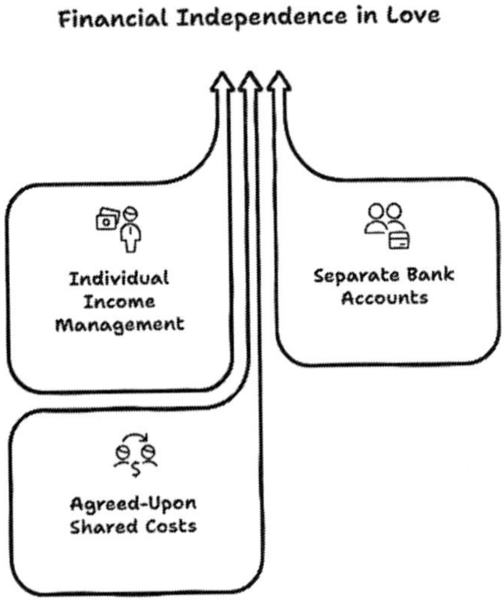

Some couples believe that love doesn't mean losing yourself, especially when it comes to money. For them, keeping finances separate isn't a sign of distance, but a way of maintaining personal clarity and reducing friction.

The Fully Separate Accounts system is exactly what it sounds like:

Each partner maintains their own bank account, manages their own income and expenses, and contributes to shared household costs in an agreed-upon manner. There is no shared or joint account in use.

Who is this ideal for?

- Couples who value financial independence and personal freedom
- Partners with very different money habits or spending styles
- Individuals who have had past experiences of financial control or trauma
- Couples in second marriages or later-in-life relationships, where financial assets are already established

This model often appeals to:

- Dual-income couples
- Entrepreneurs or freelancers with irregular incomes
- Couples who met later in life or after establishing separate careers

Benefits of Fully Separate Accounts

1. Autonomy and Freedom
   Each person has full control over their money, how they earn it, spend it, save it, and give it. There's no need to explain every purchase or ask for agreement.
2. Fewer Arguments Over Small Expenses

No more debates about "Why did you buy that?" or "Do we really need this?" Each person decides for themselves, reducing daily financial friction.

3. **Protects Individual Financial Goals**

   One partner may want to save aggressively, while the other may prioritize experiences. Separate accounts allow both to pursue their own priorities without guilt or conflict.

4. **Simpler in Case of Breakups (or Legal Reasons)**

   In unfortunate circumstances like divorce, separate finances can reduce complications, especially if assets were kept independent from the beginning.

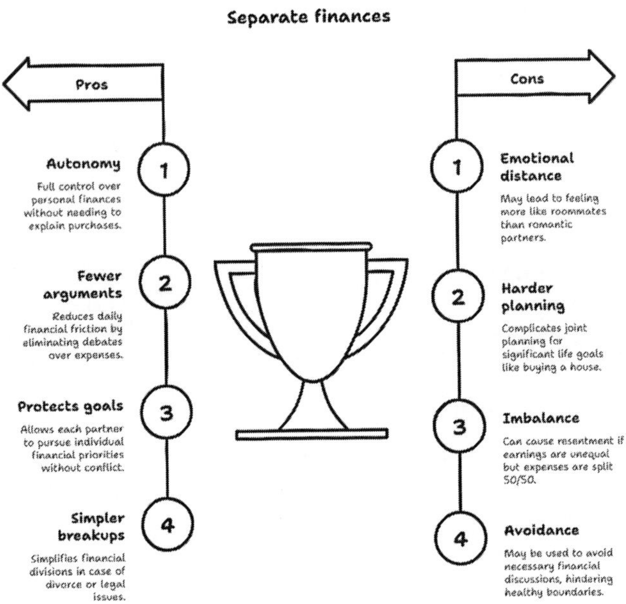

Risks and Challenges

1. Can Feel Emotionally Distant-
   When money is kept fully separate, some couples begin to feel more like roommates than romantic partners. The emotional bonding of "building something together" may be lost.
2. Harder to Plan Big Life Goals Together-
   Buying a house, having a baby, or planning for retirement requires joint vision and effort. Separate accounts can make goal-planning feel disconnected.
3. Imbalance in Lifestyle and Contributions-
   If one earns significantly more but insists on a 50/50 split, the lower earner may struggle silently or feel unfairly burdened. Resentment can grow.
4. Potential for Avoidance-
   Keeping money separate can sometimes be used to avoid tough conversations, rather than build healthy boundaries. Silence isn't the same as peace.

How to Make Separate Accounts Work Smoothly

If you and your partner prefer this system, here are some key strategies to make it healthy and fair:

1. Set Clear Contribution Agreements
   Decide how you'll share joint expenses like:
   - ❖ Rent or mortgage
   - ❖ Utilities

- ❖ Groceries
- ❖ Childcare
- ❖ Subscriptions or shared services

This can be:

- ❖ 50/50 split (if incomes are similar)
- ❖ Proportional split (if one earns more, they contribute more)
- ❖ Or even based on specific responsibilities (e.g., one pays for housing, the other covers food and transport)

2. Keep Communication Open
   Even though you don't share an account, you must share financial intentions.

   Schedule monthly or quarterly check-ins to discuss:
   - ❖ Upcoming big expenses
   - ❖ Vacations or shared plans
   - ❖ Debt repayment or savings progress

3. Respect Each Other's Spending Choices
   Each person is free to spend their money, but that doesn't mean you can ignore how it emotionally affects your partner. If one person's habits cause worry, talk about the feelings, not just the numbers.

4. Plan Joint Goals Consciously
   Use tools like:
   - ❖ Shared Google Sheets

- ❖ Money apps that track shared goals
- ❖ A mutual "goal account" if needed (for travel, wedding, home, etc.)

Even if day-to-day money is separate, your vision should still be unified.

5. Don't Use Money to Build Walls
   If separate accounts are used to hide, control, or avoid each other, pause and re-evaluate.

Healthy independence means freedom with honesty, not secrets or silence.

What If One Partner Earns Much More?

This is a sensitive spot in separate systems. A 50/50 contribution model can feel unfair when one partner is left with barely enough to save or enjoy life.

In this case:

- ❖ Consider splitting based on income percentage (e.g., 70/30)
- ❖ Or let the higher earner cover larger expenses (like rent), while the other covers smaller ones (groceries, utilities)

The key is dignity: Neither partner should feel like a burden or a benefactor.

When to Reconsider Separate Accounts

- ❖ When big life events are approaching (childbirth, home buying, elder care)
- ❖ If financial secrecy becomes a pattern
- ❖ If emotional intimacy begins to fade from money conversations
- ❖ If one partner feels left out of financial decisions or long-term planning

WAY-3

Hybrid Account System

A balance of "mine," "yours," and "ours"

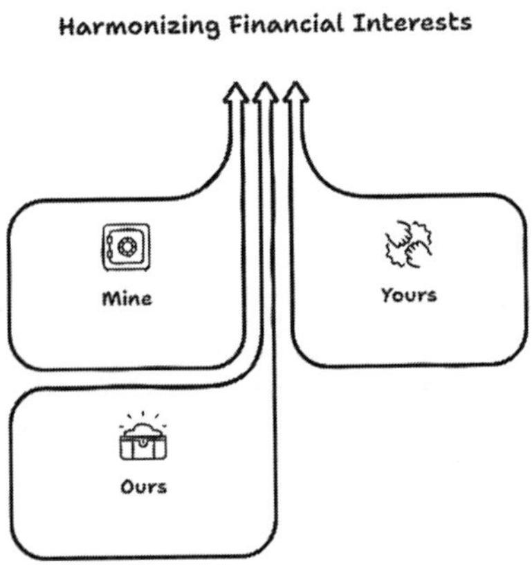

Not every couple fits neatly into the extremes of fully joint or fully separate finances. For many modern relationships, especially where both partners earn, flexibility is the key to peace, clarity, and connection.

That's where the Hybrid Account System comes in.

In this model, you create three primary accounts:

1. A Joint Account – for shared household expenses and goals
2. Partner A's Personal Account – for individual spending and savings
3. Partner B's Personal Account – for their own financial freedom

This setup allows you to function as a financial team without losing personal autonomy.

Who is this ideal for?

- Dual-income couples who want to share responsibilities but keep some independence
- Couples with different spending habits or money personalities
- Partnerships that have experienced conflict over control or judgment around money
- Those who value emotional safety *and* practical cooperation

This is now one of the most common and preferred systems among urban, working professionals in India and globally.

How It Works

1. Each partner contributes a set amount (or percentage of income) to the joint account every month.
2. That joint account is used to pay for:

- ❖ Rent/home loan
- ❖ Utilities and groceries
- ❖ Kids' expenses (if any)
- ❖ Travel or long-term savings
- ❖ Insurance, EMIs, household staff, etc.

3. The remaining money stays in each partner's personal account, to use as they choose

Benefits of the Hybrid System

1. Teamwork + Trust + Autonomy
   You're working together on shared goals, without needing to report or justify every single purchase.
2. Reduces Friction Over Small Spending
   Each person has their own space to indulge, save, or support their family, without guilt or debate.
3. Balances Income Differences Respectfully
   You can customize contributions based on who earns more, so the financial pressure doesn't fall unfairly on one partner.
4. Builds Financial Intimacy Without Sacrificing Freedom

You stay aligned on big things (home, kids, travel) while still maintaining your own identity and independence.

Risks and Challenges

1. Requires Discipline and Structure
   You'll need to sit down and agree on:
- ❖ Monthly joint expenses
- ❖ Contribution percentages
- ❖ What counts as "shared" vs. "personal" spending

2. Can Cause Resentment If Contributions Feel Unfair
   If one partner ends up feeling overburdened or the other feels financially limited, conflict can quietly build.
3. Potential for Emotional Drift
   Without regular check-ins, some couples start drifting apart in money conversations, especially if one is silently stressed or hiding financial goals or struggles.

How to Make Hybrid Accounts Work Smoothly

1. Decide on Contributions Together
   Choose from these models:
   - ❖ 50/50 Split – Only if incomes are similar
   - ❖ Proportional Split – Contribute based on income % (e.g., one earns ₹1L, one earns ₹2L → 33% + 66%)

- Fixed Contribution – Decide a fixed monthly amount each person deposits in the joint account

2. Agree on the Joint Expenses List
   What will be paid from the joint account? Be clear:
   - Daily household costs?
   - Dining out?
   - Family gifts?
   - Kids' education?

3. Set "Personal Spending Zones"
   Each partner gets freedom in their personal account—for hobbies, shopping, or sending money home, no judgment.
   Some couples also set personal saving goals: emergency funds, individual investments, or side projects.

4. Review and Adjust Every 3–6 Months
   As incomes, responsibilities, and life stages change, so should your structure. Maybe one person takes a career break. Or income goes up. Adjust contributions and goals accordingly.

5. Use Tools or Apps to Stay Aligned
   Use spreadsheets, budgeting apps, or a simple Google Doc to track:
   - Joint expenses
   - Upcoming financial goals
   - Account balances and progress

Transparency builds trust, even when money is partly separate.

When Is This System Especially Helpful?

- When one partner supports aging parents and wants privacy in managing them
- When one partner is paying off personal debt
- When both want to invest individually, at different risk levels
- When the couple wants to reduce everyday arguments about spending

Comparison of Account Systems

Characteristic	Fully Joint Accounts	Fully Separate Accounts	Hybrid Account System
Functionality	All income shared	Each partner separate	Shared and individual
Best suited	Aligned, trusting couples	Independent couples	Teamwork, freedom desired
Transparency level	Very high	Low to moderate	Moderate to high
Autonomy level	Low	Very high	Balanced
Bill management	Very easy	Requires coordination	Easy if structured
Emotional connection	Strong unity	Can feel distant	Healthy connection
Control issues risk	Higher if unequal income	Lower, potential secrecy	Low, check-ins help
Flexibility over time	Hard to adjust	Very flexible	Highly adaptable
Financial check-ins needed	Yes	Yes	Yes
Conflict triggers	May feel restrictive	Unequal lifestyle	Requires regular talks
Power dynamics risk	High if one earns more	Low, unless avoidance	Low, promotes respect
Ideal situation	Total unity desired	Value independence	Best of both worlds

Now Let's Talk About Real-Life Situations

Situation 1: Both Partners Are Earning

This is the most flexible scenario. You have options.

Ideal system: Hybrid

- ❖ Decide how much to contribute to the joint account (e.g., 50/50 or based on income ratio)
- ❖ Use personal accounts for your own expenses, hobbies, and gifts

Tip: Use the joint account for rent, bills, groceries, travel, savings, and investments.

Why it works: It balances fairness and independence.

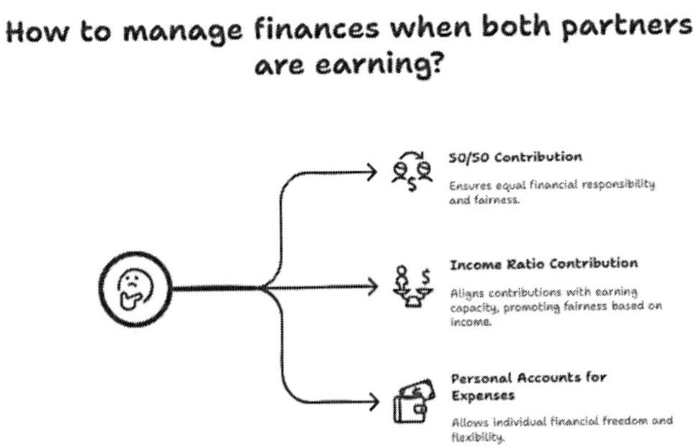

Situation 2: One Partner Earns, One Doesn't

This can be during maternity leave, a career break, caregiving, or studying.

Ideal system: Fully joint or hybrid with transparent access

Important rule:

Money should be shared, not given like pocket money.

- Non-earning partners contribute in invisible ways: emotional support, home care, family tasks
- That contribution is just as valuable as a salary

How to make it work:

- Have one joint account for all shared expenses
- Give both partners equal access and agency
- Personal spending budgets can still be allowed to maintain dignity and independence

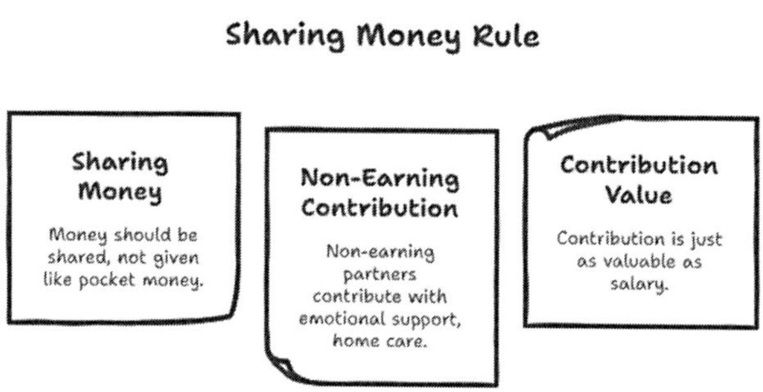

Situation 3: Big Income Difference Between Partners

This is common and totally okay. The goal isn't equality in numbers. It's fairness in impact.

Ideal system: Hybrid with percentage-based contribution

- For example: One earns ₹1 lakh/month, the other ₹40,000/month
- Instead of splitting 50/50, they contribute 60% and 40% to the joint account

Why it works:

It removes guilt from the lower earner and pressure from the higher earner. Both feel respected.

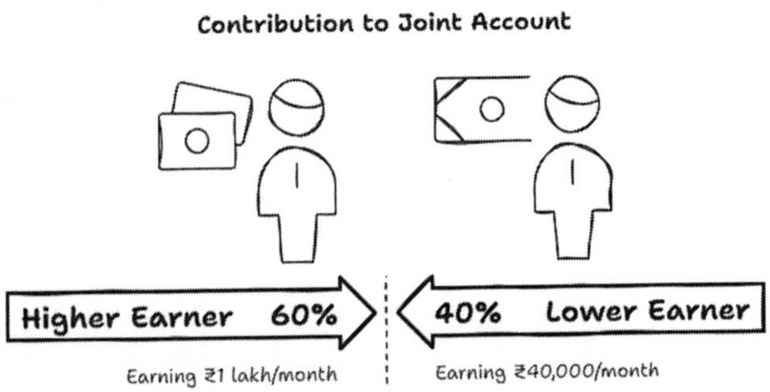

Situation 4: One Partner Is a Business Owner or Freelancer

Income may be irregular, but that doesn't mean finances have to be.

Ideal system: Hybrid with flexibility

- ❖ Set a monthly base contribution to the joint account
- ❖ In higher-income months, contribute more to shared goals or emergency funds

Bonus tip:

Make room for business expenses in personal accounts, not joint.

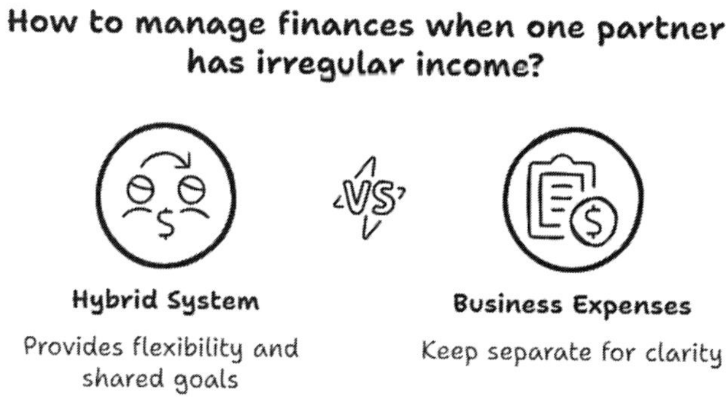

Situation 5: Long-Distance or Working in Different Countries

Exchange rates, currencies, and the cost of living can complicate things.

Ideal system: Joint savings goal + individual accounts

- ❖ Use a shared digital tracker to plan big goals (relocation, wedding, home)

❖ Each partner contributes in a way that's fair in local terms

Tip: Set a "contribution in spirit" rule, not just currency.

Mini Quiz: What's Your Couple Money Style?

Find the Right Account Setup for Your Relationship

Answer the following questions individually or together. Tally your scores at the end to see which money style may suit you best.

1. How do you feel about financial independence in a relationship?
   A. I value having my own money for personal choices. (3 points)
   B. I'm okay sharing everything, we're a team. (1 point)
   C. I want both: shared goals + personal freedom. (2 points)

2. When it comes to tracking expenses…
   A. I like to keep an eye on my own budget. (3 points)
   B. I prefer us to have full visibility of everything, together. (1 point)
   C. I want shared tracking for joint expenses, but freedom with my own spending. (2 points)

3. How do you handle big income differences?
   A. I think everything should be proportional to what each person earns. (2 points)
   B. It doesn't matter, I'm happy to carry more or less, as long as we're together. (1 point)
   C. I think we should each be able to contribute, but also retain some independence. (3 points)

4. How do you feel when your partner spends money without telling you?
   A. It's fine if it's their own money. (3 points)
   B. I'd prefer we talk about all spending, big or small. (1 point)
   C. I'm okay with personal spending as long as joint responsibilities are covered. (2 points)

5. What do you value most in a financial partnership?
   A. Freedom and autonomy (3 points)
   B. Trust and complete transparency (1 point)
   C. Balance and clarity (2 points)

Add up your score:

A) 5–7 points:

You're most comfortable with a Fully Joint Account system.

You value shared responsibility and feel safest when everything is visible and together.

B) 8–12 points:

You're best suited to a Hybrid System: Joint + Personal accounts.

You care about shared goals but also want some space and independence.

C) 13–15 points:

You prefer Fully Separate Accounts with clear agreements.

You thrive when you have financial freedom and clarity on your own terms.

Next Step: Discuss Your Results

Ask your partner:

- What felt true in this quiz?
- What are we already doing well?
- Where can we improve how we manage our money?

The goal isn't to "match answers," it's to understand and support each other's money personalities.

Chapter 5

From Birth to School Fees

Planning for a Child, Emotionally, Practically, and Financially

Bringing a child into your life is one of the most meaningful choices a couple can make, and one of the most financially demanding. From planning for medical expenses to investing for their education, the decisions you make today will echo for decades.

This chapter is divided into two key phases:

1. **Pre-Child Financial Planning– Preparing for the arrival: emotionally, practically, and monetarily.**
2. **Post-Child Adjustments– How your budget, priorities, and financial strategy evolve after the baby is born.**

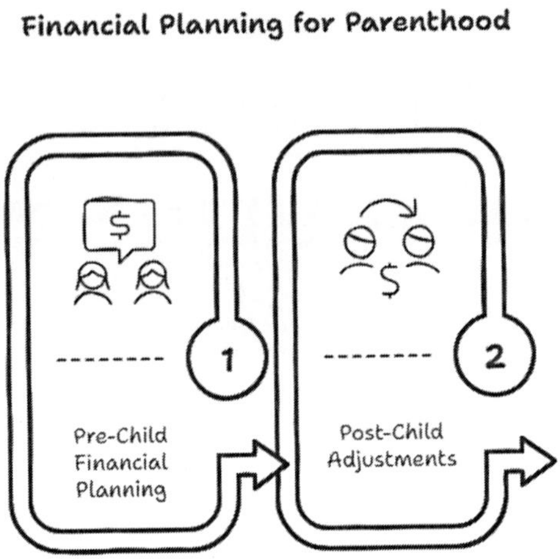

Phase 1: Financial Planning Before Having a Child

1. Have the Conversation First

Before you think cribs and baby names, talk money:

- ❖ Are we both emotionally and financially ready?
- ❖ Can we sustain a single income for a while, if needed?
- ❖ Do we need to relocate, change jobs, or reduce debt before starting?

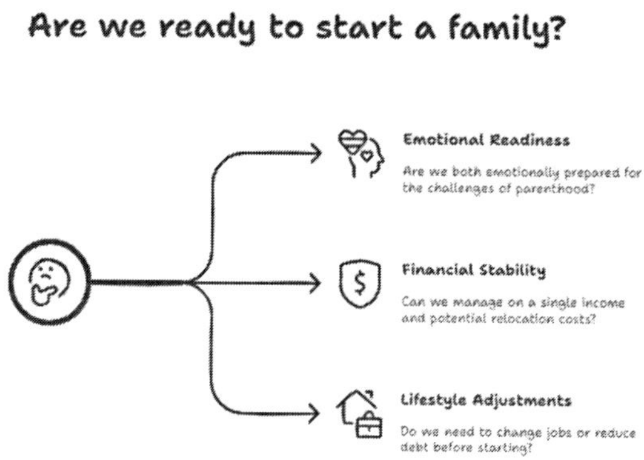

2. Estimate the Early Expenses

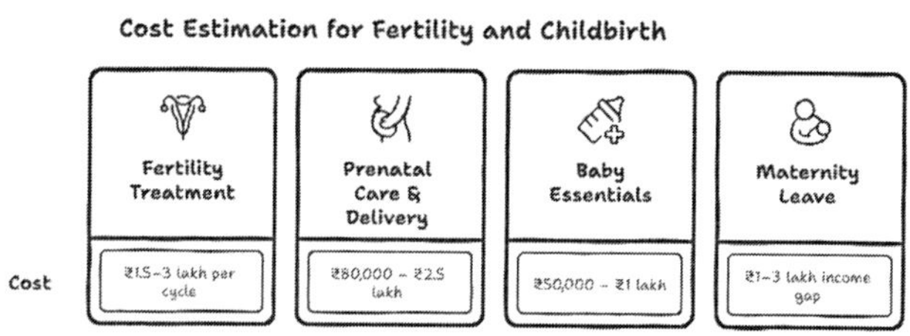

Planning for pre-child expenses requires a clear view of major cost areas in the initial phase. Fertility treatments like IVF or IUI can cost between ₹1.5–3 lakh per cycle, while prenatal care and delivery in a private hospital may add another ₹80,000 to ₹2.5 lakh. Setting up for the baby—including essentials like a crib, stroller, clothes, and other items—can range from ₹50,000 to ₹1 lakh. Additionally, if maternity leave is unpaid or partially paid, families may face an income gap of ₹1–3 lakh. In total, prospective parents should aim to save around ₹4–9.5 lakh to comfortably cover these early expenses without financial stress.

Tip: Build a liquid emergency fund of at least 6–12 months' household expenses, including maternity/ paternity leave coverage and any medical contingencies

3. Where to Invest for Pre-Child Goals (0–3 Years Horizon)

For pre-child goals with a short investment horizon of 0 to 3 years, safety and liquidity take priority over high returns. For hospitalisation, delivery, and initial setup costs, instruments like liquid funds, ultra-short-term debt funds, and bank fixed deposits are ideal, as they offer low risk, though with limited protection against inflation.

If you're saving for a fertility treatment corpus, recurring deposits or arbitrage funds can be considered, balancing low to moderate risk while still offering limited inflation protection. For building an emergency fund, options like sweep-in fixed deposits or liquid mutual funds are most suitable, given their very low risk and relatively better inflation protection compared to traditional savings avenues.

Investment Options Comparison

	Hospitalisati on/Delivery	Fertility Treatment	Emergency Fund
Instruments	Liquid Funds	Recurring Deposit	Sweep-in FD
Risk	Low	Low to Moderate	Very Low
Inflation Protection	Limited	Limited	Moderate

Phase 2: How Children Change the Money Equation

Once the baby arrives, your money map changes. Your priorities pivot, life insurance, education planning, and budgeting take center stage.

Once the baby arrives, couples should prepare for a significant rise in monthly expenses. In urban areas, essential items like diapers, formula, and hygiene products can cost between ₹4,000–₹8,000 per month. Healthcare-related costs, including vaccinations and regular pediatric visits, may add another ₹1,500–₹3,000.

If childcare support is needed, daycare or nanny services can range from ₹8,000–₹20,000 monthly. While some savings may occur due to reduced dining out or travel, estimated at ₹5,000–₹10,000 a month, these are usually outweighed by the new expenses. On balance, couples should expect a net additional monthly outflow of approximately ₹8,500 to ₹21,000, and plan their budgets accordingly to maintain financial stability.

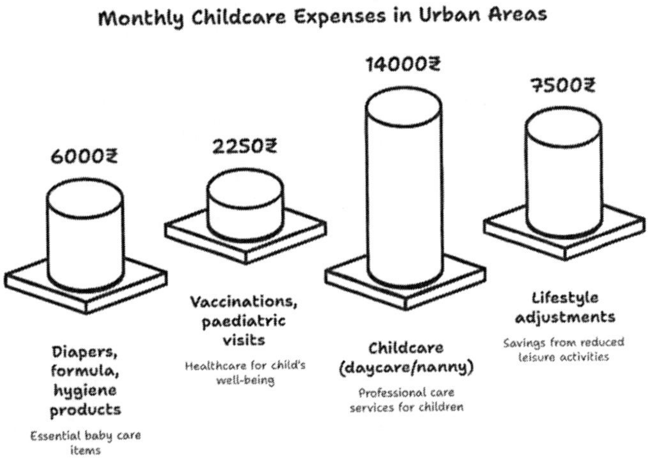

Rebuild your budget to align with this new chapter. Use expense tracking tools (like Walnut, ET Money, or YNAB India-style sheets) to spot leaks and adjust.

2. Insurance is Now Essential

Term Life Insurance: Each earning partner should have a pure term plan worth at least 15–20x annual income.

(Example: If your income is ₹10 lakh/year, aim for ₹1.5–2 crore cover.)

Health Insurance: Ensure a family floater plan covering both parents and the newborn. Opt for ₹10–15 lakh coverage with maternity benefits if planning ahead.

Critical Illness/Disability Insurance: These are often overlooked but can be life-saving.

3. Education Planning: Begin Early

By the time your child is 18, a 4-year undergraduate degree could cost upwards of ₹50–60 lakh at a private college in India or ₹1.5–2 crore for overseas education, factoring in 7–10% annual inflation.

Investment Options Comparison

Characteristic	School Fees	College Corpus	Girl Child	Backup Education Fund
Horizon	3–10 years	10–18 years	0–15 years	5–10 years
Instrument	SIPs in Balanced Advantage or Hybrid Funds	Equity Mutual Funds (SIPs), PPF	Sukanya Samriddhi Yojana (SSY)	Index Funds (Nifty 50, Sensex), Flexi-cap Funds
Notes	Lower volatility than pure equity	Equity for growth, PPF for tax-free safety	7.5–8% tax-free returns, only for girl child	Good for diversified growth

When planning for a child's education, aligning each goal with the right investment horizon and instrument is key. For school fees over a 3–10-year period, SIPs in Balanced Advantage or Hybrid Funds are ideal, offering moderate growth with lower volatility than pure equity. For building a college corpus over 10–18 years, Equity Mutual Funds through SIPs provide long-term growth potential, while adding PPF offers tax-free stability. For a girl child, the Sukanya Samriddhi Yojana (SSY) is a highly recommended option, offering attractive 7.5–8% tax-free returns with a 15-year horizon. Additionally, a backup education fund can be built over 5–10 years using Index Funds like Nifty 50 or Sensex, or diversified Flexi-cap Funds, ensuring a safety net for future educational needs.

Have discussed more about it in case studies; you will have an idea.

Action Plan for Couples

1. Pre-baby Checklist:
   - Create a ₹3–5 lakh baby corpus
   - Buy or upgrade insurance policies
   - Check health coverage for maternity inclusion
   - Start a small SIP for long-term child goals
2. Post-baby Adjustments:
   - Redesign your budget every 6 months
   - Automate investments toward school/college goals
   - Name the child as a nominee in key policies/accounts
   - Update wills and financial documents

Final Thoughts

A child doesn't just change your life; they change how you define financial success. It's no longer about returns or status, but stability, protection, and purpose. The sooner you prepare, the more confidently you can focus on what truly matters, raising a healthy, happy child.

Case studies you should DEFINITELY read –

Amit and Neha's Journey to Financial Parenthood

Amit and Neha, a couple in their early 30s living in Pune, reached out to me with a familiar question:

"We want to have a baby next year, but we're worried, can we afford it?"

They had a combined monthly income of ₹1.5 lakhs (Amit earned ₹85,000 and Neha earned ₹65,000), ₹6 lakhs in total savings, and typical living expenses of around ₹75,000 per month. Like many middle-class Indian couples, they were managing well, but planning for a child meant stepping into unfamiliar territory.

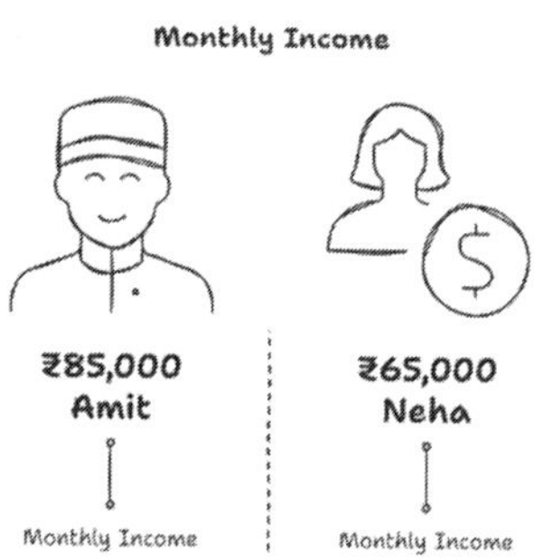

Phase 1: Pre-Baby Planning – Building the Foundation

When we first spoke, they were unsure where to start. Together, we broke their child-planning journey into manageable parts.

Here's the plan we made:

1. Estimate Costs:
    - ❖ Maternity care and delivery (private hospital): ₹1.5–2.5 lakh
    - ❖ Baby setup (crib, stroller, clothes, etc.): ₹60,000
    - ❖ Emergency buffer: ₹1–1.5 lakh
    - ❖ Potential income gap during Neha's maternity leave: ₹1.5 lakh

2. Create a Dedicated Baby Fund:
    - ❖ We set up a liquid fund SIP of ₹10,000/month, plus they moved ₹1 lakh from an FD into this fund. This would comfortably build a ₹3–3.5 lakh corpus in 8–10 months.

3. Insurance Review:
    - ❖ Amit took a term life insurance plan for ₹1.5 crore (₹900/month).
    - ❖ Neha upgraded their family health insurance to ₹10 lakh, with maternity coverage built in.

4. Start Long-Term Investing Early:
    - ❖ Neha had a PPF running; she increased contributions to ₹5,000/month.
    - ❖ We launched a ₹3,000 SIP in a Balanced Advantage Fund, earmarked for future school fees.

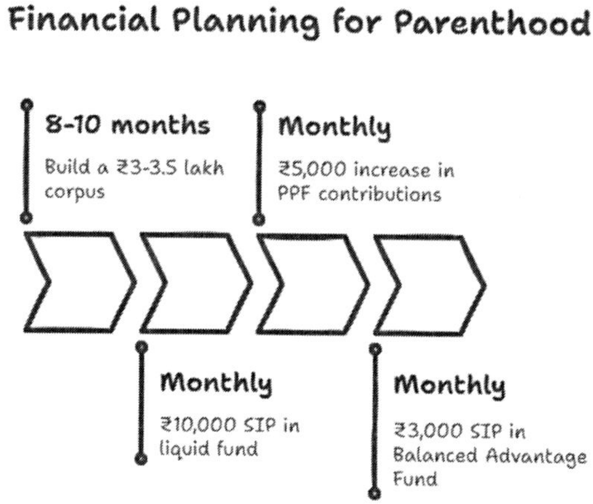

Phase 2: Post-Baby Adjustments – Adapting with Ease

Aarav was born 11 months later, and Neha took a 4-month break from work. Their household income dipped temporarily to ₹85,000/month, but their baby fund helped bridge the gap.

What changed after the baby arrived:

Monthly expenses rose by ₹12,000–₹14,000, mostly in baby care and medical visits.

- We paused their SIPs for 3 months during the transition, then resumed them slowly as Neha returned part-time.
- Shifted ₹2 lakh from the baby fund into a short-term debt fund, keeping it safe yet liquid.

We also revised their investment plan:

The revised investment plan aims to balance short-term needs and long-term goals with a structured, goal-based approach. For immediate financial security, ₹2 lakh is allocated to a liquid fund as an emergency buffer.

To build a future education corpus, a monthly SIP of ₹5,000 is directed into an Equity Flexi-cap Fund, offering growth potential over the long term.

Recognizing the need for school fees in the next three years, a relatively safer SIP of ₹3,000 per month is invested in a hybrid fund, which balances equity and debt exposure. Additionally, if the couple plans to have a second child, the Sukanya Samriddhi Yojana is being considered to secure the girl's future, although contributions have not yet started.

Investment Planning

Goal	Strategy	Amount
Emergency fund	Liquid Fund	₹2,00,000
Education corpus	SIP in Equity Flexi-cap Fund	₹5,000/month
School fees (starting in 3 years)	SIP in Hybrid Fund	₹3,000/month
Girl child future (if planning second child)	Consider Sukanya Samriddhi Yojana	Not started yet

Reflections: What Amit and Neha Learned

Amit told me, “We thought we weren’t ready. But this plan gave us confidence. It felt like we were preparing for a new life, financially and emotionally.”

Neha added, “Having clear numbers made the whole process feel less overwhelming. I could enjoy my pregnancy instead of stressing over costs.”

Lessons for You

- ❖ Planning a baby isn’t about being rich, it’s about being prepared.
- ❖ Starting early, even with modest SIPs, helps you stay ahead of education inflation.
- ❖ Revisit your financial plan every 6–12 months as your child grows and needs change.

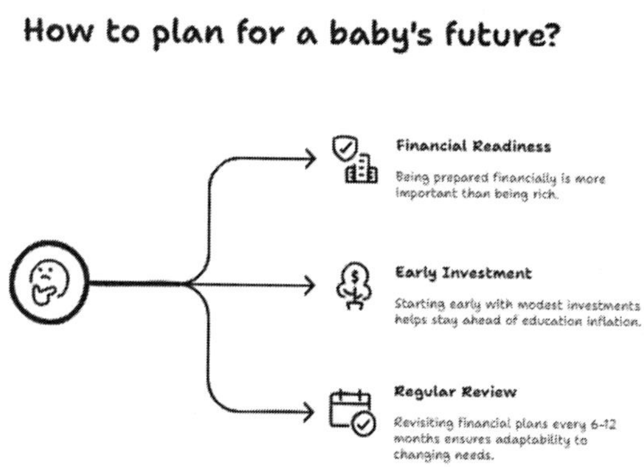

Pro tip for couples:

You don't have to figure it all out alone. Like Amit and Neha, sometimes a simple conversation with a guide can turn fear into a roadmap.

Case study 2

Case Study: Priya's Solo Income, Smart Strategy

Planning a child on a single income with purpose and precision

Priya, a 29-year-old schoolteacher from Jaipur, reached out to me with a quiet kind of worry:

"My husband and I want to have a child next year, but I'm the only one earning right now. Is it even possible to manage everything on ₹60,000 a month?"

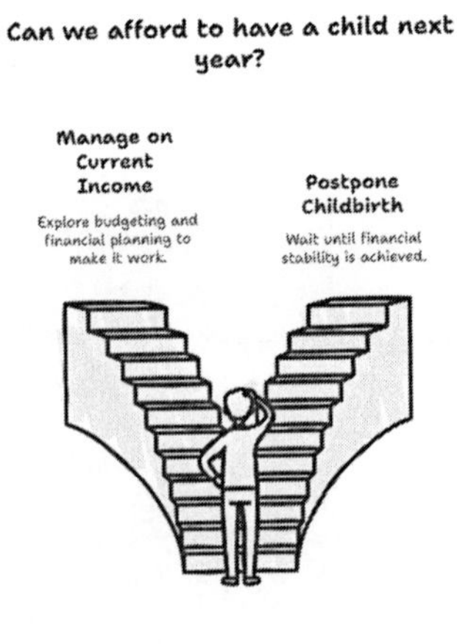

Her husband was preparing for government exams and had paused work temporarily. Their savings stood at ₹4 lakhs, with no major debt but tight monthly expenses.

Phase 1:

Planning on One Income, Getting Creative with Constraints

When we began working together, Priya assumed she needed to delay their family plans by 3–5 years. But with a clear, cautious, and consistent approach, we created a plan that helped her feel in control without cutting corners.

Here's how we structured it:

1. Redefine Priorities and Set a Timeline
   - ❖ Target baby planning 12–15 months ahead to allow time for saving.
   - ❖ Minimize lifestyle inflation: pause vacation plans, cut discretionary spending (\~₹5,000/month saved).
2. Build a Baby Emergency Fund
   - ❖ Shifted ₹1.5 lakh from their FD into a liquid mutual fund.
   - ❖ Started a SIP of ₹5,000/month in the same fund to reach ₹2 lakh+ in 12 months.

3. Secure the Family with Protection First
    - ❖ Bought a term plan of ₹1 crore for Priya (₹700/month).
    - ❖ Upgraded health insurance to a ₹10 lakh family floater with maternity benefit.

4. Keep Long-Term Goals in Sight
    - ❖ Opened a PPF account with ₹3,000/month contributions, safe, tax-free, long-term.
    - ❖ Added a ₹1,000 SIP in a conservative hybrid fund for school planning (starting small, to scale later).

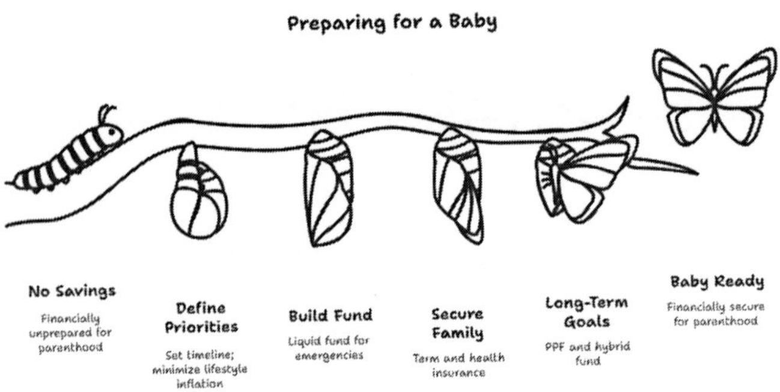

Phase 2: Adjusting Post-Delivery, Lean and Flexible

Their daughter, Meher, was born the following year. Priya took 3 months of unpaid maternity leave, during which their household ran solely on their savings and emergency fund.

Changes after the child:

❖ Monthly expenses increased by ₹8,000–₹10,000 (baby care, doctor visits).

❖ Paused PPF and SIPs temporarily for 4 months, resumed when her salary stabilized.

❖ Shifted ₹1 lakh into an ultra-short-term debt fund to keep money accessible yet growing.

Financial Goals and Strategies

Goal	Strategy	Payment Type
Emergency fund	Liquid Fund	₹2 lakh corpus
Term Insurance	₹1 crore cover	₹700/month
Education (long-term)	SIP in Equity Hybrid Fund	₹1,500/month
Short-term buffer	Ultra-short Debt Fund	₹1 lakh

Priya's Takeaway

Priya told me, "At first, I thought we just couldn't afford to be parents yet. But breaking it down into small steps gave me hope, and a plan."

What changed most was her mindset. From anxious to empowered. From postponing parenthood out of fear to stepping into it with purpose.

Lessons for Other Single-Income Families

- ❖ You don't need a 6-figure salary, you need structure, discipline, and realism.
- ❖ A longer runway (12–15 months) gives you time to prepare without stress.
- ❖ Start small with SIPs. Focus first on insurance and emergency funds before chasing returns.

Your role as the guide:

You showed Priya that being financially ready isn't about how much you earn; it's about how well you plan. That's the power you're giving readers throughout this book.

Chapter 6

Emergency Funds and Financial Safety Nets: Preparing for the "What Ifs" as a Couple

Life is unpredictable. What if one of you loses your job? What if there's a medical emergency, or your bike needs major repairs? What if a family member needs financial help all of a sudden?

These "what ifs" can hit hard, and that's where an emergency fund becomes a lifesaver. It may not be glamorous like investing in mutual funds or buying gold, but it's your first line of defense in any financial crisis.

Think of an emergency fund like your financial "rainy-day dabba," quietly sitting in a corner, ready to help when the storm comes.

How should we prepare for financial emergencies?

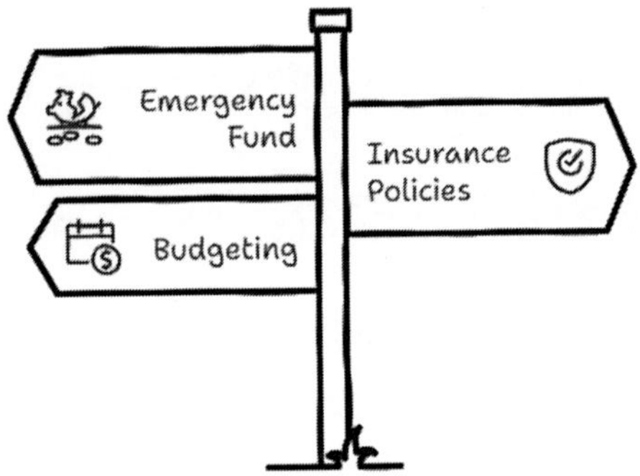

Why Couples Need a Financial Safety Net

We don't just manage money for ourselves; we often support parents, siblings, or even extended family. That's part of our culture. But it also means that when emergencies strike, the financial pressure can be intense.

Without a safety net, even a small crisis, like a sudden hospitalization, job loss, or house repair, can feel like a mountain. And when money is tight, tempers can rise. Couples may end up arguing, blaming, or withdrawing. But with a financial cushion in place, you can focus on solving the problem together, not just surviving it.

What Is an Emergency Fund (And What It's Not)

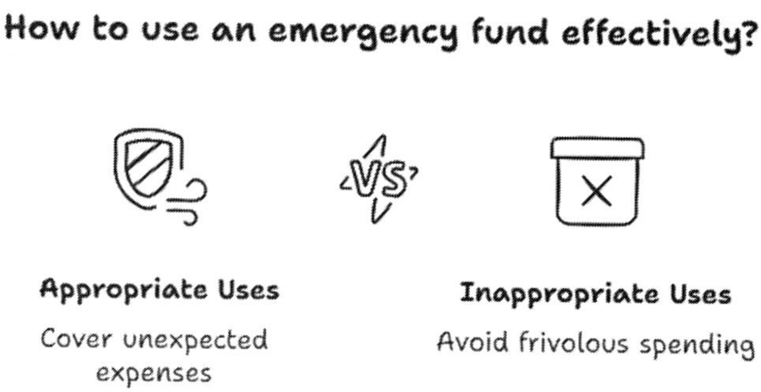

An emergency fund is money you keep aside only for unexpected, urgent situations. It's not for your cousin's wedding gift, your Goa trip, or a new phone on EMI.

It should be:

- Easy to access – Like a savings account or a fixed deposit with a low penalty for withdrawal.
- Meant only for emergencies – Think hospital bills, job loss, car/bike breakdown, or urgent home repairs.
- Enough to cover 3 to 6 months of basic expenses – Rent, groceries, school fees, EMIs, electricity bills.

Can't save that much right away? That's okay. Even ₹10,000 to start with is better than nothing. Build it slowly.

How Couples Can Build an Emergency Fund

1. Talk About Your "What Ifs"
   What are your biggest fears: job loss, medical emergencies, business slowdowns? Talk about them openly. A teacher and a freelance designer will have different risks, just like a salaried couple in Mumbai will have different needs than a small-town business couple.
2. Decide on a Number Together
   Calculate your essential monthly expenses. Multiply that by three. That's your minimum goal. It's okay if it takes time, just keep going.
3. Choose the Right Place to Park It
   Keep it in a joint savings account or a short-term fixed deposit. Apps like Paytm Money or banks like SBI, HDFC, and ICICI make this easy. Avoid risky options like stocks or mutual funds for this fund.
4. Set Up an Auto Transfer
   Decide on an amount, ₹1,000, ₹2,000, or even ₹500, and auto-transfer it every month after your salary hits. Treat it like a non-negotiable bill.
5. Agree on What Counts as an Emergency
   Define this before the crisis hits. A health scare? Yes. IPL tickets or Diwali shopping? Definitely not.
6. Celebrate Small Wins
   When you hit ₹10,000, then ₹25,000, acknowledge it. Maybe go out for a dosa or a chai date, not to spend, but to appreciate the teamwork.

Other Safety Nets to Consider in India

Emergency funds are just the start. Here are other things couples should think about:

Insurance and Backup Options

Characteristic	Health Insurance	Term Life Insurance	Accident/Critical Illness	Gold and FDs
Purpose	Covers medical expenses	Provides financial security after death	Covers accidents and critical illnesses	Acts as emergency backup fund
Importance	Essential due to rising costs	Vital if one partner is main earner	Key for travelers, physical jobs	Helpful when quick money needed

Emotional Security = Financial Security

When you build a safety net together, it's not just about the money. It's about feeling protected as a team. It tells both of you, **"We're ready. Whatever comes our way, we've got each other's backs."**

And that's the kind of security no FD or gold coin can give.

In a Nutshell:

- Emergency funds help couples stay calm when life throws a surprise.
- Start small, stay consistent, and define what an "emergency" really means for you.

- ❖ In India, where extended family and responsibilities are part of the package, a safety net gives you control, and confidence.
- ❖ It's not just financial planning, it's future-proofing your relationship.

Case Study 1: Asha and Kunal – When Life Took an Unexpected Turn

City: Pune
Profession:
Asha – school teacher;
Kunal – sales executive
Monthly Income: ₹65,000 combined

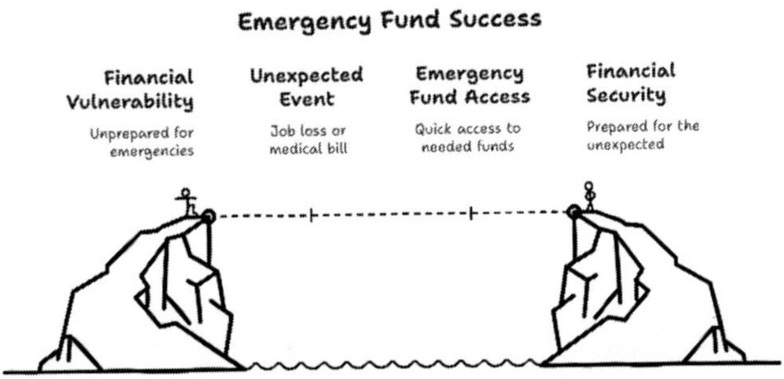

I first met Asha and Kunal during a young couples' financial literacy workshop I conducted in Pune. They were newly married, full of dreams, and focused on buying their first home within five years. While they were

excited about investing in SIPs and saving for a house, they didn't see the need for an emergency fund.

"I don't think anything major will happen," Kunal had said casually.

But Asha, practical and thoughtful, took my advice seriously. I had shared a simple emergency fund planner with them and encouraged them to start small. They committed to saving ₹3,000 a month in a separate savings account. It wasn't a big step, but it was a powerful one.

Fifteen months later, I got a message from Asha. Kunal had met with a road accident. His leg was fractured, requiring surgery and weeks of bed rest. While his employer's health insurance covered a part of it, there were co-payments, recovery costs, and the shock of a temporary loss in income.

But they didn't panic.

They had ₹45,000 in their emergency fund. It helped them pay for his treatment, manage rent and groceries, and get through those uncertain weeks without falling into debt or asking for help.

Asha told me:

"That one fund saved our peace of mind. We could focus on Kunal's healing, not on our bills."

I felt like someone who had quietly helped two people stay strong through life's storms.

Case Study-2

Nisha and Raghav – Parenthood, Pandemic, and Planning Ahead

City: Lucknow

Profession: Nisha – freelance graphic designer; Raghav – private bank employee

Monthly Income: ₹80,000 combined

I started working with Nisha and Raghav a year before the pandemic. They were thoughtful, cooperative, and expecting their first child. During one of our sessions, I had introduced the idea of an emergency fund.

At first, they hesitated. "We're already saving for delivery costs," Raghav said. "Isn't that enough?"

But I gently explained the difference between planned and unplanned expenses. What if income dropped suddenly? What if the baby needed unexpected medical care? Eventually, they agreed to build an emergency fund, ₹3,500 a month, into a liquid mutual fund.

They saved ₹1.2 lakh over three years.

When COVID-19 struck in early 2020, the world turned upside down. Raghav's salary was slashed, and Nisha's freelance projects were paused indefinitely. Their baby arrived during lockdown. Hospital bills, medicines, and newborn care all piled up.

But they never borrowed. Never defaulted. Never panicked.

They dipped into the emergency fund and survived those difficult months with grace. They even helped Raghav's retired parents financially when their pension got delayed.

Later, Raghav sent me a message I'll never forget:

"You didn't just help us save money. You gave us control when everything else felt out of control."

That's when I knew this is what emergency funds are really for. Not just protection, but peace.

Conclusion

I've seen markets rise and fall. But what affects people the most are the unplanned moments life throws at them. These two stories remind me, and hopefully, you TOO, that an emergency fund is not just a financial buffer. **It's a source of emotional strength, dignity, and freedom.**

And in a country like India, where extended family, health costs, and job instability are real concerns, every couple deserves this layer of protection.

Chapter 7

Insurance: Love, and Liability

Life, health, disability, and how to protect each other when it matters most.

When most couples talk about money, they usually think about spending plans, savings goals, or investments. Insurance is rarely part of the conversation until life throws a curveball. But here's the truth: insurance is not just about risk, it's about love. It's how you protect each other when things go wrong. It's how you say, "Even if I'm not okay, you will be."

In this chapter, let's break down the three key types of insurance every couple must talk about: life insurance, health insurance, and disability insurance. I'll explain what they are, when you need them, how much you need, and the common mistakes to avoid.

Insurance Types

Life Insurance	Health Insurance	Disability Insurance
Provides financial security to beneficiaries upon death.	Covers medical expenses for illness or injury.	Replaces income if you can't work.

Life Insurance: Love That Lives On

Because protecting your loved ones is the ultimate form of love.

What Is Life Insurance?

Life insurance is a financial contract in which an insurance company agrees to pay a lump sum, called the death benefit, to your nominee if you pass away during the policy term.

This money can help your spouse or children manage their lives without facing a financial crisis.

It's not about expecting death—it's about ensuring life continues smoothly for your loved ones, even if you're not there to support them.

You insure your car or phone, why not your income, which is the foundation of your family's financial well-being?

Why Couples Need Life Insurance

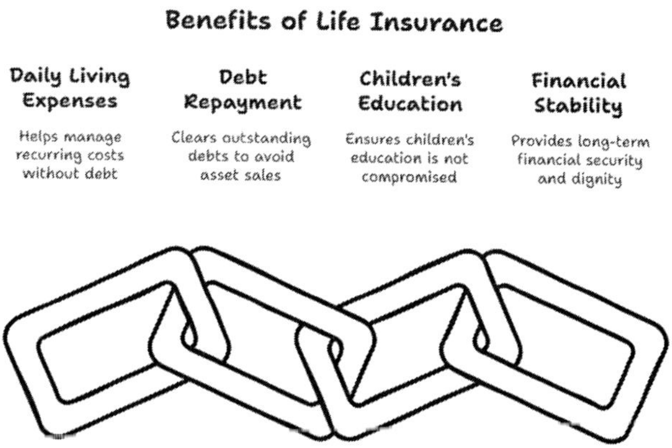

When you're single, your financial responsibilities are limited. But once you're married or in a long-term relationship, your finances become deeply interconnected.

If something were to happen to one of you, the other may still be responsible for shared loans, household expenses, and children's needs. That's why life insurance is essential.

Let's break it down:

1. To Cover Daily Living Expenses

If one partner is a homemaker or earns less, the loss of the primary breadwinner can create significant financial stress.

Life insurance helps the surviving partner manage rent, groceries, utilities, school fees, and other recurring expenses without falling into a debt trap.

2. To Pay Off Debts

In many Indian households, couples take joint home loans, car loans, or personal loans. If one partner passes away, the entire repayment responsibility shifts to the other.

A term insurance payout can be used to immediately clear all outstanding debts, so the surviving partner isn't forced to sell assets or depend on family.

3. To Fund Children's Education

Raising a child is expensive. From school fees to college and higher education, costs can easily run into lakhs.

Life insurance ensures that your child's future doesn't get compromised due to the absence of one parent.

4. To Maintain Financial Stability

Beyond daily expenses, your partner needs to plan for long-term financial stability. Insurance gives them the financial freedom to grieve and heal without financial panic. It helps maintain their dignity and way of life during a difficult time.

What Kind of Life Insurance Should You Get?

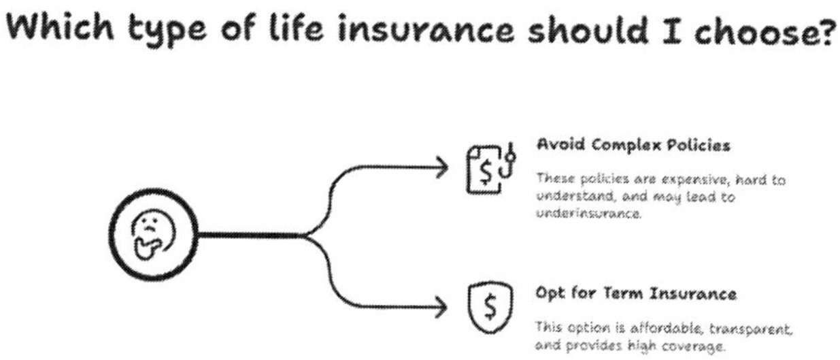

There are several types of life insurance in the market. However, not all are suitable for everyone.

Avoid Complex Investment-Linked Policies

Plans like endowment policies or ULIPs combine insurance with investment. These are often expensive, come with high charges, and are difficult to understand. Most people end up underinsured with these plans.

Unless you fully understand how they work and are comfortable with their long lock-ins and low returns, it's best to avoid them.

Opt for Term Insurance

Term insurance is pure protection. It's simple, cost-effective, and offers a large cover at an affordable premium.

Key benefits:

- Affordable: High coverage at a low premium.
- Transparent: No investment or savings element.
- Focused: Pays only on death during the term.

Example: A healthy 30-year-old can get ₹1 crore term cover for under ₹1,000 per month.

Use mutual funds or PPF for your investments. Use term insurance for protection. Don't mix the two.

How Much Life Cover Do You Need?

Use this basic formula:

Life cover = 10 to 15 times your annual income + liabilities + future financial goals

Step 1: Income Replacement

If you earn ₹10 lakh annually, your family would need ₹1 crore to ₹1.5 crore to replace your income for the next 10 to 15 years.

Step 2: Add Liabilities

Include all outstanding loans, home loans, personal loans, car loans. For example, if you have a ₹40 lakh home loan and a ₹5 lakh car loan, that's ₹45 lakh added to your required cover.

Step 3: Add Future Responsibilities

Consider your children's education, aging parents' care, and spouse's long-term financial support.

Example:

- Income: ₹10 lakh per year
- Liabilities: ₹45 lakh
- Children's future expenses: ₹30 lakh Recommended cover: ₹1.5 crore to ₹2 crore

Other Important Tips

Buy Early

The earlier you buy, the lower your premium. Insurers consider your age and health. Once your premium is locked in, it remains the same for the entire term. Start as early as possible, ideally in your twenties or early thirties.

Don't Wait Until You Have Children

If you're planning to have children in the near future, your insurance needs will grow significantly. Buy term insurance now so you are well-covered when your family expands.

Add Riders for Extra Protection

Riders are optional benefits you can add to your term insurance plan. Useful riders include:

- Critical Illness Rider: Pays a lump sum if you're diagnosed with a severe illness like cancer or a heart attack.
- Accidental Death Benefit: Provides an additional sum if death occurs due to an accident.
- Waiver of Premium: If you become disabled or critically ill and can't work, future premiums are waived, but your policy continues.

These riders offer additional security at a small extra cost.

Real-Life Example

Rajeev and Neha, a couple from Bengaluru, were expecting their second child. Rajeev, 34, earned ₹14 lakh per year. Neha was a homemaker. They had a ₹50 lakh home loan.

When they came to me, they had no life insurance. We calculated their needs and helped Rajeev buy:

- ₹2 crore term insurance
- Critical illness rider worth ₹25 lakh
- Accidental death benefit rider
- Nominee: Neha

Now, if anything were to happen to Rajeev, Neha would be financially secure, the home loan would be paid off, and the children's education would be funded. Most importantly, she wouldn't have to depend on others or compromise on lifestyle.

Couple Life Insurance Checklist

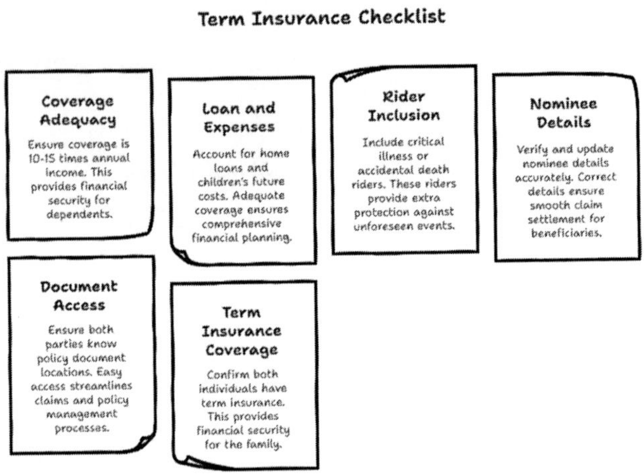

Use this checklist to make sure both of you are adequately protected:

- Do both of us have term insurance?
- Is the cover amount at least 10–15 times our annual income?
- Have we accounted for home loans and children's future expenses?
- Are riders like critical illness or accidental death included where relevant?
- Are the nominee details updated?
- Do both of us know where the policy documents and login details are stored?

Life insurance isn't a product, it's a promise.

A promise that says, "Even if I'm not around, you'll be okay."

When couples build a future together, they must also protect that future. Life insurance gives you the peace of mind that no matter what happens, your partner and children will have financial support to carry on.

Because real love doesn't end with life, it lives on through care, protection, and planning.

Health Insurance: When Sickness Strikes, You're Covered

Because illness shouldn't break your bank or your spirit.

What Is Health Insurance?

Health insurance is a financial product that pays for your medical expenses when you fall sick or get injured. Depending on the policy, it may cover:

- Doctor consultations and fees
- Hospitalization (room rent, nursing charges)
- Surgeries
- Diagnostic tests
- Medicines and treatment
- Pre- and post-hospitalization expenses

Some plans even include ambulance charges, daycare procedures, and home treatment, depending on the insurer.

In short, it protects your health and your wallet.

Why Couples Need Health Insurance

Benefits of Health Insurance for Couples

Characteristic	Protects Savings	Access to Treatment	Reduces Stress
Financial Impact	Prevents depletion of savings	Enables quality care at reputed hospitals	Alleviates monetary concerns during illness

In today's world, a single hospitalization can cost ₹1 lakh to ₹5 lakh or more—even in middle-tier hospitals.

Medical inflation in India is rising at 10–15% annually. That means every year, the cost of treatment gets more expensive.

Here's why health insurance is a must for couples:

1. Protects Your Savings

Without health insurance, even a minor surgery or prolonged illness can wipe out your emergency fund or force you into debt. Insurance allows you to get the required treatment without touching your long-term savings or investments.

2. Access to Better Treatment

With insurance, you're not forced to choose the cheapest hospital or delay treatment due to cost. You can go to reputed network hospitals and get quality care.

3. Reduces Financial Stress

When someone in the family is seriously ill, emotional stress is already high. Financial stress can make things worse. Health insurance lets you focus on recovery, not money.

Types of Health Plans for Couples

There are mainly two ways couples can structure their health coverage:

Comparing health insurance plans based on coverage flexibility.

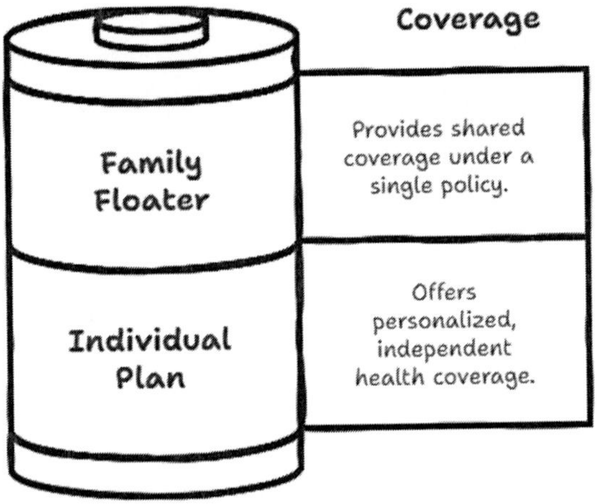

1. Individual Health Plans

Each partner has a separate policy with their own sum insured. For example, both husband and wife have individual policies of ₹10 lakh each.

Pros:

- Higher total coverage
- Claims by one person don't affect the other's sum insured
- Useful if one partner has pre-existing conditions

Cons:

- Slightly higher premium compared to a floater for young, healthy couples

2. Family Floater Plan

A single policy that covers both partners under one sum insured. The cover can be used by either person or shared as needed. You can also add children or parents later.

Pros:

- Lower premium compared to two individual plans
- Easier to manage (one renewal, one claim process)
- Suitable when both partners are young and healthy

Cons:

- If one person uses a large portion of the cover, less is left for the other
- Premium increases sharply with age or if one partner makes multiple claims

Which One Should You Choose?

- If both partners are **under 40 and healthy**, a **family floater** can be more affordable and convenient.
- If one partner has **health issues or is over 45**, **individual policies** offer better protection.

How Much Health Cover Should You Have?

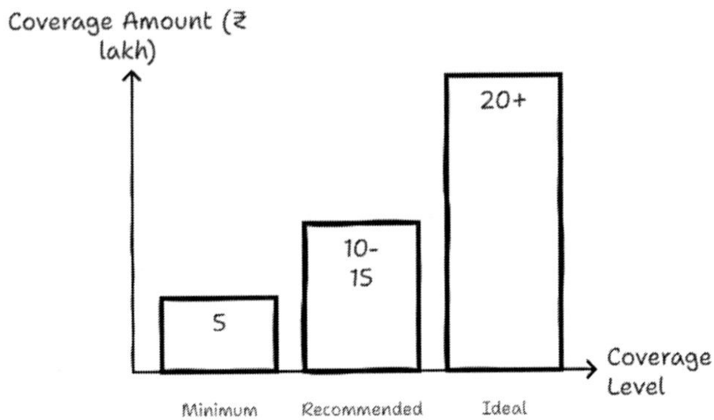

Health Insurance Coverage Recommendations

In cities like Mumbai, Delhi, or Bengaluru, a single hospital stay for a major condition can cost ₹3 to ₹7 lakh.

Here's a practical rule of thumb:

- **Minimum**: ₹5 lakh per person (only for young, healthy couples in Tier 2 cities)
- **Recommended**: ₹10 to ₹15 lakh cover (for couples in metros or with dependents)
- **Ideal**: ₹20 lakh+ base plan with a **top-up** or **super top-up** of ₹50 lakh to ₹1 crore

What is a Super Top-Up Plan?

It's an add-on policy that kicks in when your base policy is exhausted. It offers large coverage at low premiums and is a smart way to increase protection.

What to Check Before Buying Health Insurance

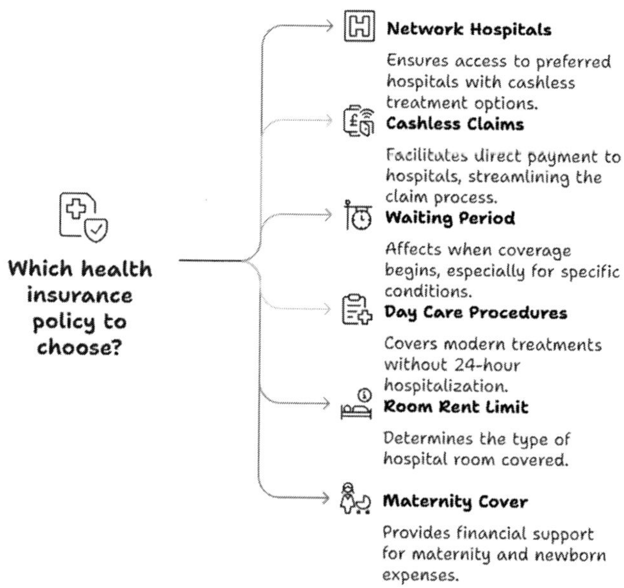

All policies are not the same. Here are key things to watch out for:

1. Network Hospitals

Make sure the insurer has a wide list of hospitals in your city. Check if your preferred hospital is in the **cashless network**—this allows you to get treated without paying upfront.

2. Cashless Claim Facility

With cashless claims, the insurer pays the hospital directly. Always choose a plan with a strong and fast claim settlement process.

3. Waiting Periods

Many policies have waiting periods:

- 30 days for general illnesses
- 1–2 years for specific treatments
- 2–4 years for **pre-existing diseases**
- 2–3 years for **maternity** cover

Choose a policy with shorter waiting periods if possible.

4. Day Care Procedures

Many modern treatments, like cataract surgery or chemotherapy, don't need 24-hour hospitalization. Ensure your policy covers **daycare procedures**—ideally 500 or more.

5. Room Rent Limit

Some policies cap the hospital room rent (e.g., ₹5,000/day). Choose plans with **no room rent sub-limits** or with a **private single room** eligibility.

6. Maternity and Newborn Cover (if planning a family)

Some plans cover maternity and newborn expenses after a waiting period of 2 to 4 years. If children are in your near-future plans, get a policy with maternity benefits early.

Pro Tip: Don't Rely Only on Employer Insurance

Many couples assume their company-provided group policy is enough. But:

- It ends when you leave the job
- It usually has lower coverage (₹3–5 lakh)
- It may not cover dependents adequately

Always buy a **personal, portable** health insurance policy. This stays with you regardless of job changes, layoffs, or retirement.

Case Example from My Practice

Amit and Shweta, a couple from Pune in their early 30s, had employer health coverage but no personal plan.

When Shweta needed emergency gallbladder surgery, her company's insurance rejected part of the claim due to hospital limits.

They had to pay ₹1.8 lakh from savings.

Later, I helped them purchase:

- A ₹15 lakh family floater health plan
- A ₹50 lakh super top-up policy
- Maternity cover, as they were planning their first child

Now they are well-covered, with peace of mind.

Couple's Health Insurance Checklist

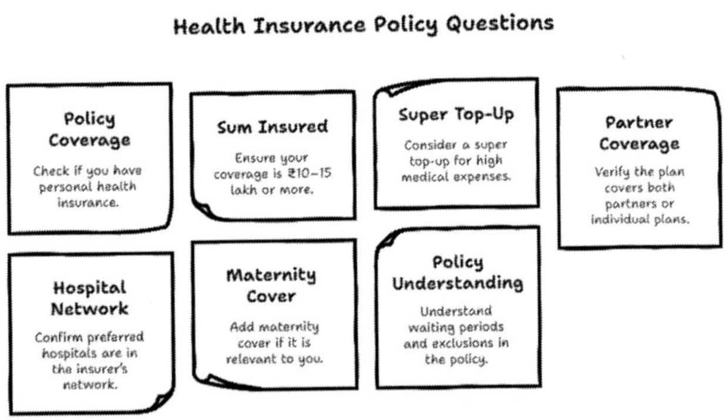

Use this to check if your health coverage is adequate:

- Do we have a personal health insurance policy?
- Is our sum insured ₹10–15 lakh or more?

- Do we have a super top-up for high expenses?
- Does the plan cover both partners (or are we on individual plans)?
- Are our preferred hospitals part of the insurer's cashless network?
- Have we added maternity cover if relevant?
- Do we understand the waiting periods and exclusions?

Health is unpredictable. But your finances don't have to be.

Health insurance protects your savings, gives you access to quality care, and brings peace of mind in moments of crisis. As a couple, your goal is to grow together, not be financially derailed by one illness.

Take a policy when you don't need it, so that when you do, it's already there for you.

Because in sickness and in health, true financial planning always stands by your side.

Disability Insurance: Income Protection When You Can't Work

What is it?

If an illness or accident leaves you unable to work (temporarily or permanently), disability insurance gives you a portion of your income regularly.

Why couples need it:

We insure our lives, but we forget to insure our ability to earn. If one partner becomes disabled and can't work, it can cause:

- ❖ Loss of income
- ❖ Strain on the other partner's finances
- ❖ Long-term impact on goals like buying a house, raising kids, or retirement

There are two kinds:

- ❖ Temporary disability insurance (for short-term illness or injury)
- ❖ Permanent disability insurance (for long-term or lifelong disability)

Some life and health insurance policies offer accidental permanent disability riders, but they're not always enough. A dedicated income protection plan is better.

How much cover do you need?

Ideally, the payout should replace 60–70% of your monthly income, especially if you're the main earner.

Who needs it most?

- ❖ Freelancers and self-employed professionals (no paid sick leave!)

- ❖ High-income earners with large responsibilities
- ❖ Couples with EMIs and dependents

What Should Couples Do?

Here's what I tell every couple I advise:

- ✓ Sit down together and list all your current insurance policies
- ✓ Check the coverage amount—is it enough for your current life stage?
- ✓ Review the nominee's name—update them after marriage or having kids
- ✓ Don't just rely on employer-provided plans—buy personal policies
- ✓ Set reminders for policy renewals
- ✓ Talk to a trusted advisor if you're unsure

Insurance isn't just paperwork. It's a form of love, quiet, powerful, and practical. It's how you say to your partner:

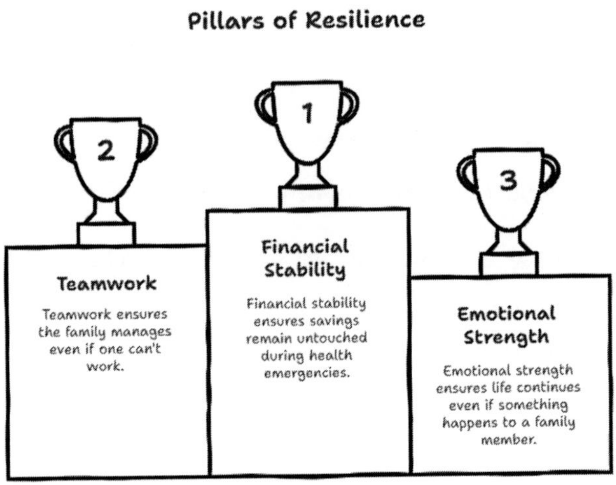

"Even if something happens to me, your life won't fall apart."

"Even if we face a health emergency, we won't have to drain our savings."

"Even if I can't work, we'll still manage as a team."

You build wealth to live well. But you buy insurance so you don't lose what you've built.

So don't avoid this topic. Talk about it. Act on it.

Because in love and in money, protection is a promise.

Chapter 8

Retirement Planning as a Couple

From solo dreams to shared visions, how to retire together, not apart.

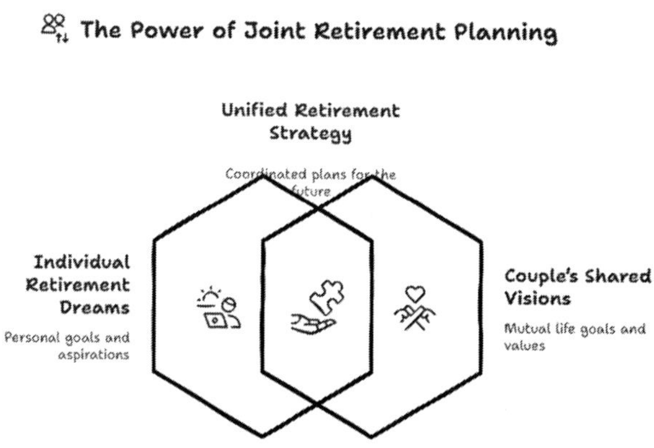

Retirement is not the end of your story; it's the beginning of a new chapter. For couples, it's an opportunity to finally enjoy time together without work pressures, deadlines, or school admissions. But this phase can also bring anxiety if you're not financially aligned or emotionally prepared.

Some couples drift apart during retirement, not because they don't love each other, but because they never talked about what retirement means to each of them.

This chapter is about making sure you don't just retire, you retire together.

Why Retirement Planning is a Couple's Job

In India, retirement has often been viewed as an individual journey. The husband retires, gets a pension. The wife adjusts. Or vice versa.

But that mindset is outdated.

Whether you're dual-income or one of you is a homemaker, planning retirement together ensures:

- No surprises about money or expectations
- Emotional connection through shared dreams
- Balanced finances that protect both of you
- A peaceful lifestyle you both enjoy

Building a Harmonious Retirement

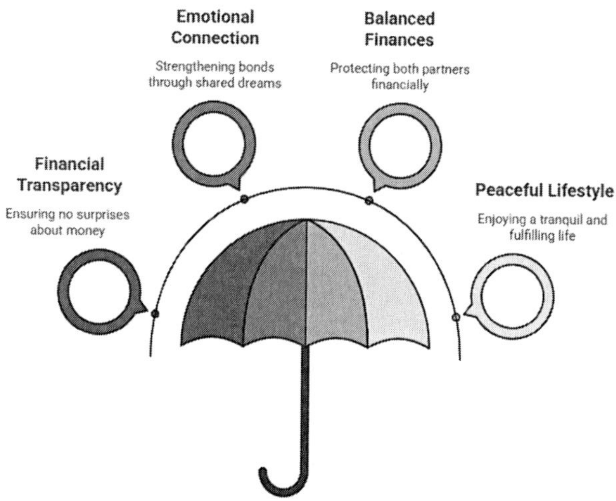

HOW MUCH MONEY IS NEEDED TO RETIRE?

There's no magic number that fits everyone, but a practical and widely accepted rule of thumb is that you should retire with at least 25 times your annual expenses saved. This is based on the assumption that you'll live around 25 to 30 years post-retirement, and that your money needs to outpace inflation while providing a steady income. Let's break it down with a relatable example.

Suppose a couple currently earns ₹1 lakh per month and spends around ₹70,000 monthly. That means their annual expenses today are approximately ₹8.4 lakh. Using the 25x rule:

₹8.4 lakh × 25 = ₹2.1 crore

This is the minimum corpus they need at the time of retirement to maintain their current lifestyle.

But here's the twist: this ₹8.4 lakh will not remain the same. Thanks to inflation (which in India ranges between 6–7% annually for living expenses), the cost-of-living doubles approximately every 10–12 years. So, if this couple is 40 today and plans to retire at 60, their current ₹70,000 monthly expenses could grow to around ₹1.4–1.6 lakh/month by the time they actually retire. That pushes their annual expenses to roughly ₹18–20 lakh per year at age 60.

Impact of Inflation on Cost of Living

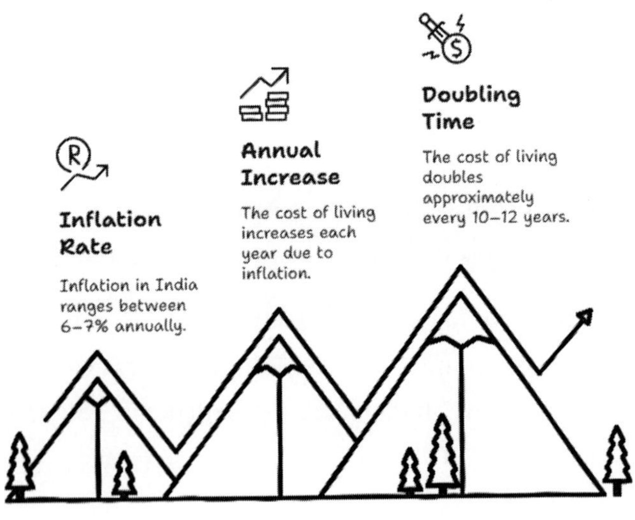

Recalculating with inflation-adjusted expenses:

₹20 lakh × 25 = ₹5 crore

So, in today's rupees, ₹2.1 crore sounds okay—but adjusted for future inflation, the retirement corpus should actually be closer to ₹4–5 crore if you want to retire comfortably at 60 and live until 85–90 without financial stress.

This corpus is meant to cover everything: daily living, medical expenses, emergencies, travel, and even a little fun. It also assumes you'll invest your retirement funds in a balanced way post-retirement, so that while you're withdrawing from it, a portion continues to grow (at a rate higher than inflation).

The bottom line? Plan not just **for today's lifestyle**, but for tomorrow's prices. Retirement planning isn't just saving; it's protecting your future lifestyle against time and rising costs.

Age-Wise Retirement Savings Milestones (as a Couple)

Planning for retirement can feel overwhelming, but breaking it down into age-based savings goals makes it manageable.

This chart offers a simple rule of thumb: by certain ages, you and your partner should aim to have saved a multiple of your annual household income. These milestones help ensure you're on track for a financially secure retirement.

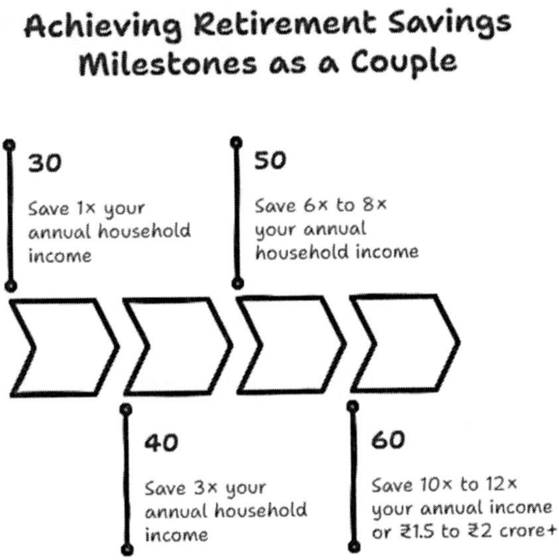

- By Age 30: You should aim to have saved at least your full annual income. For example, if your combined annual income is ₹10 lakh, you should have ₹10 lakh saved for retirement. This includes EPF, PPF, NPS, mutual funds, etc.
- By Age 40: Your goal increases to three times your income. If you earn ₹12 lakh a year, you should target ₹36 lakh in retirement savings.

- By Age 50: As retirement nears, your savings need to accelerate. You should aim for 6 to 8 times your annual income. For instance, with an income of ₹15 lakh, your savings should be between ₹90 lakh to ₹1.2 crore.
- By Age 60: You're nearing or entering retirement. Ideally, you should have 10 to 12 times your income saved, or at least ₹1.5 to ₹2 crore+, depending on your lifestyle and expected expenses.

Why These Milestones Matter:

- They give you a clear benchmark at each stage of life.
- Help couples align their savings strategies and stay motivated.
- Avoid last-minute financial stress or dependence on children in old age.
- These targets are based on average inflation, life expectancy, and post-retirement spending in India.

Financial Planning Pyramid

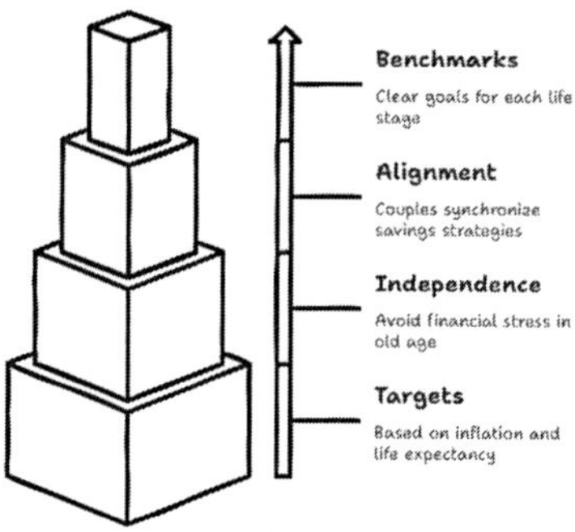

How can one reach these targets?

Investment plans and options for retirement –

Follow the table below, these kinds of investments may help you with your retirement.

Diversified plan based on risk and time

Characteristic	25–30 years	10–20 years	0–10 years
Primary Focus	Growth	Balanced	Safety
Suggested Instruments	High risk mid cap funds, equity, index funds	Equity + Debt Mutual Funds, NPS, EPF, PPF	Combination of debt funds, hybrid funds, flexi cap funds

Some other safe investments for those who can't take the risk in the stock markets.

Couple-Friendly Retirement Investment Options:

Investment Option	Ideal For	Returns (Approx.)	Lock-in Period	Tax Benefit	Risk Level	Notes / Tips
EPF / VPF	Salaried couples	~8% (tax-free)	Till retirement/job switch	Section 80C	Very Low	Employer match boosts savings; VPF is a voluntary top-up
PPF	All couples	~7.1% (tax-free)	15 years	Section 80C	Very Low	Open separate accounts for each spouse; ideal for stability
NPS	Long-term goal planners	9–11% (varies)	Till age 60	80C + ₹50k extra (CCD 1B)	Moderate	Auto or active asset choice; tax-efficient pension plan
Mutual Fund SIPs	Wealth-building couples	10–14% (equity)	No lock-in (ELSS: 3 yrs)	ELSS under 80C	Medium to High	Go for flexi-cap, index, or hybrid funds; review annually
REITs / Real Estate	Couples seeking assets	6–9% (average)	Medium to long-term	Limited (loan-related, etc.)	Medium	REITs are liquid; physical property requires active mgmt.
SCSS	Retired couples (60+)	~8.2%	5 years (extendable)	Section 80C	Very Low	Offers safe, monthly income post-retirement

Understanding Risk and Reward in Retirement Investments

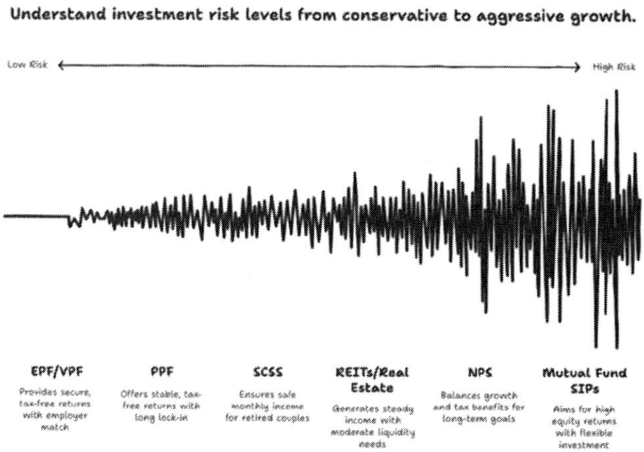

The Basic Rule: Risk = Potential Reward

There's a universal truth in investing:

The lower the risk, the lower the return. The higher the risk, the higher the potential return.

(Follow the graph above to understand the risk and reward of investments.)

Investment Strategy

Characteristic	Long Term	Medium Term	Short Term
Time Horizon	20+ years	10–20 years	10 years
Risk Tolerance	High	Moderate	Low
Asset Allocation	70–80% Equity, 20–30% Debt/PPF	50–60% Equity, 40–50% Debt/PPF/NPS	20–30% Equity, 70–80% Debt/SCSS/FDs

Retirement investing is a marathon, not a sprint.

The earlier you start, the more risk you can take, and the higher the potential reward. Time is your strongest ally.

How to generate a passive source of income for retirement:

Now that you've built a solid retirement corpus, the next challenge begins: **turning that wealth into regular income** that supports your lifestyle, healthcare, and dreams in your golden years.

Retired couples no longer earn a salary, but they still need predictable monthly cash flows. There are several popular instruments designed to generate retirement income; some offer safety, others offer returns, and a few offer both.

Let's explore the common options retirees consider for regular income, and understand why **Systematic Withdrawal Plans (SWPs)** from mutual funds often stand out as the most **balanced, flexible, and tax-efficient solution**.

Why SWP Can Be the Smartest Way to Get Regular Income

SWP (Systematic Withdrawal Plan) is a simple but powerful tool that lets you withdraw a fixed amount monthly from your mutual fund investment.

Think of it like creating a monthly salary from your own wealth, but smarter.

SIP-SWP Cycle

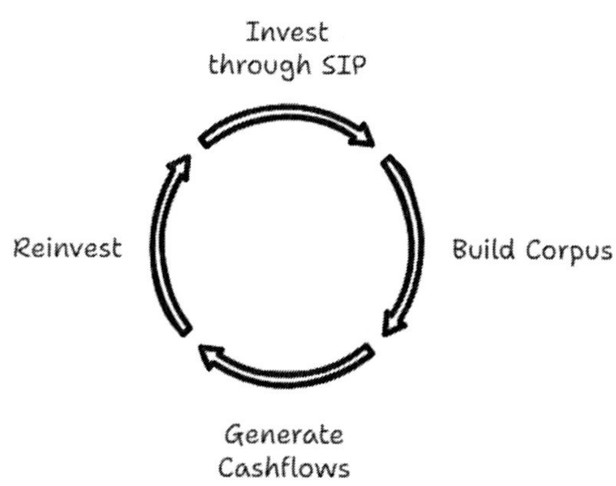

Other instruments you should know for retirement plans to generate monthly cash flows

1. **Senior Citizen Savings Scheme (SCSS)**

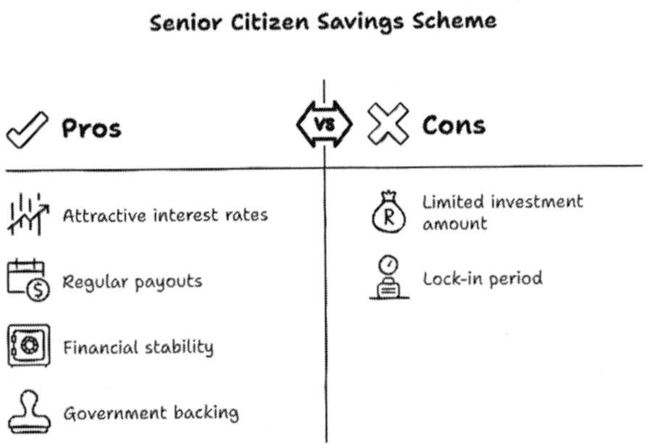

What it is:

A government-backed scheme with fixed interest, available for citizens above 60.

Why it's great:

Assured returns (currently ~8.2% per annum)

Interest paid quarterly

Government guarantee

Ideal for: Safe and fixed-income seekers

Max limit: ₹30 lakhs (as of FY 2024-25)

2. PMVVY (Pradhan Mantri Vaya Vandana Yojana)

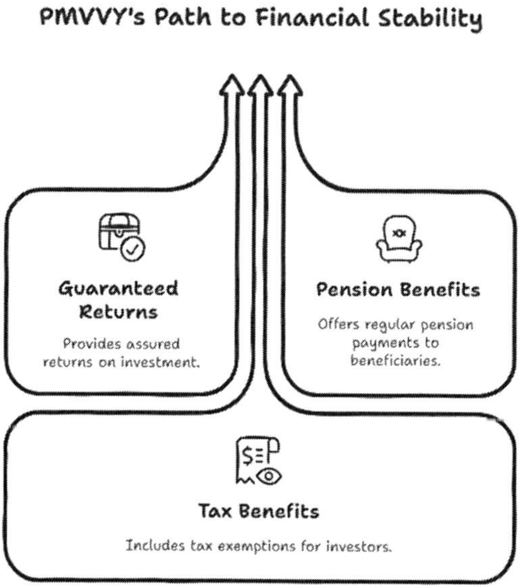

What it is:

A pension scheme run by LIC for senior citizens.
Why it's great:
Assured pension for 10 years
Interest rate ~7.4% (changes yearly)
Monthly/Quarterly/Annual payout options

Ideal for: Retired couples wanting a predictable, guaranteed pension

3. Monthly Income Schemes (Post Office MIS)

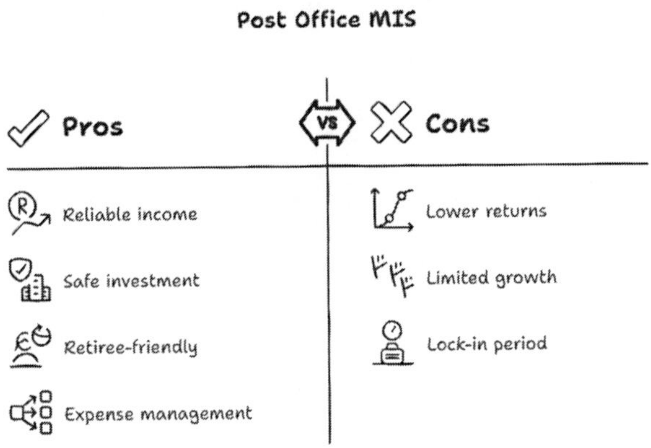

Monthly Income Schemes (Post Office MIS)

What it is:

A small savings scheme from India Post that pays monthly interest.

Why it's great:

Fixed monthly payout

Low risk

Government-backed

Max limit: ₹9 lakhs (individual), ₹15 lakhs (joint)

Current rate: ~7.4% annually (paid monthly)

4. Rental Income

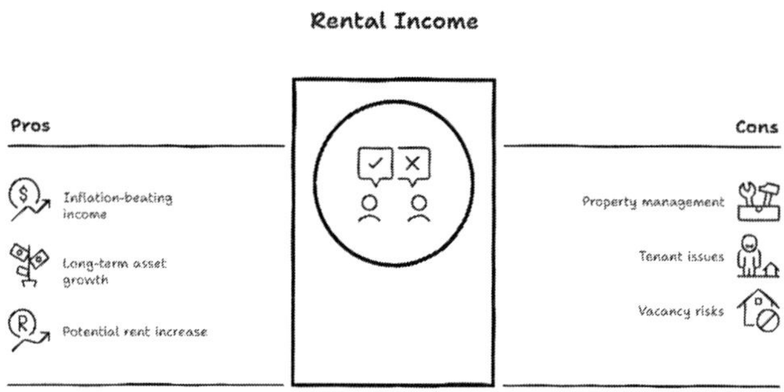

What it is:

Earning rent from property (residential or commercial).

Why it's great:

Inflation-beating income

Long-term asset growth

Can increase rent over time

Keep in mind: Property management, tenant issues, vacancy risks

Ideal for: Those who already own property

5. Dividend Income from Stocks/Mutual Funds

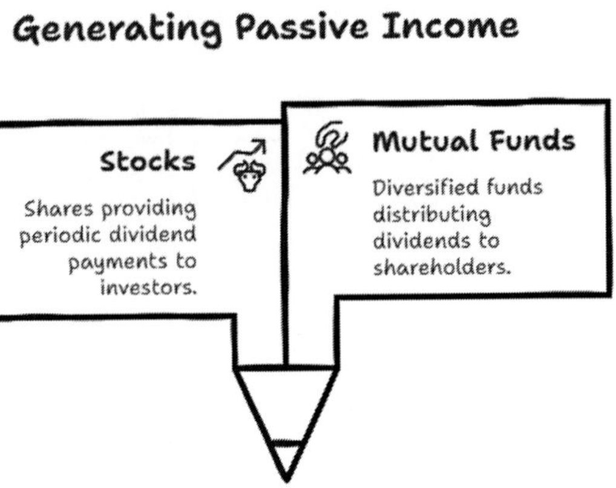

What it is:

Companies or mutual funds pay out a share of profits regularly.

Why it's great:

Passive income

Potential for portfolio growth

Not guaranteed; depends on company performance

Ideal for: Couples with investment knowledge or a financial advisor

Why SWP Is One of the Best Options

Benefits for You and Your Spouse

Benefit	Meaning
Regular Cash Flow	Fixed monthly amount credited to bank
Higher Returns	Beat inflation with mutual funds
Flexible	Change amount or stop anytime
Tax Efficient	Taxed only on growth, not withdrawal
Joint Planning	Invest jointly, nominate each other

Real Example – How SWP Works at Scale

Let's say you and your spouse have retired with a corpus of **₹1.5 crore** and want to generate a steady monthly income through a **Systematic Withdrawal Plan (SWP)**. You invest this amount in a balanced mutual fund that offers an assumed average return of **10% annually**.

You decide to withdraw ₹1 lakh per month (₹12 lakh per year) to cover your living expenses.

Year	Starting Corpus	Annual SWP (₹1L/ month)	Returns @10%	Corpus at Year End
1	₹1,50,00,000	₹12,00,000	₹15,00,000	₹1,53,00,000
2	₹1,53,00,000	₹12,00,000	₹15,30,000	₹1,56,30,000

Even after withdrawing ₹24 lakh over two years, your corpus still grew by ₹6.3 lakh!

What This Means for You:

- Your lifestyle is funded with ₹1 lakh/month, without touching the principal.
- Your retirement corpus not only survives—it continues to grow.
- Over a 20–25-year retirement, this strategy can offer a sustainable income stream without the fear of running out of money too soon.

Final Thoughts: Retirement Is a New Beginning, Not an End

Retirement doesn't mean the end of earning. It simply means your money starts working for you instead of you working for money.

As a couple, your retirement years should be about peace, freedom, and fulfillment, not stress about monthly bills or market uncertainty. That's why planning for regular, predictable income is so important.

Among all the tools available, government schemes, fixed deposits, annuities, and Systematic Withdrawal Plans (SWPs) stand out for one simple reason:

They combine the comfort of a monthly income with the power of long-term growth.

Why SWP Works So Well for Retired Couples

- It turns your mutual fund investment into a monthly paycheck.
- You decide how much and when you want to withdraw.
- Your remaining money continues to grow in the market, helping you beat inflation.
- It's flexible no lock-ins, no penalties if you want to change your plan.

Pros
Monthly income
Flexible withdrawals
Inflation beat
No lock-ins

In short, SWP is simple, smart, and sustainable, a perfect fit for couples who want to enjoy retirement without worrying about money running out.

Your Golden Years, Your Way

With the right planning, your retirement can be a time of connection, joy, travel, and legacy-building. Whether it's living comfortably, supporting your family, or giving back to society, income planning makes it all possible.

You've spent decades building your wealth together. Now it's time to spend it wisely, together.

Part 3

Outside Forces and High Stake Decisions

Chapter 9

Family Pressure and Cultural Expectations

When your wallet has more than two people in it.

Family Pressure and Cultural Expectations.

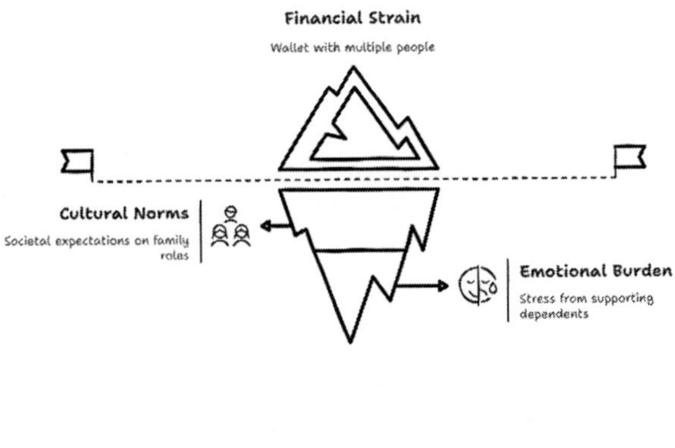

The Unseen Expense: Expectations

In India, money is rarely just between two people, especially after marriage. From helping parents and siblings to funding weddings and festivals, couples often face unspoken expectations that shape their financial lives.

These aren't "bad" things. They're part of our love, our culture, and our identity. But if not handled wisely, they can become silent stressors that chip away at both wealth and the relationship.

In this chapter, we'll explore how family pressures and cultural norms impact couples' finances, and how couples can respect traditions without compromising their own future.

What Family Pressure Looks Like

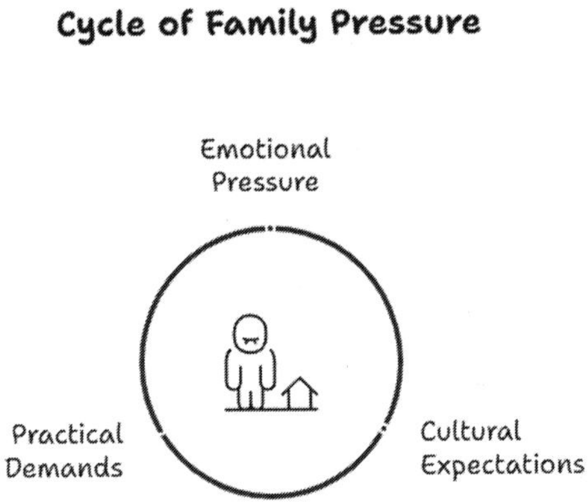

Family pressure can be emotional, cultural, or even practical. Some common scenarios include:

- ❖ Monthly support to elderly parents
- ❖ Funding a sibling's education or marriage
- ❖ Hosting grand religious functions or festivals
- ❖ Taking over the family business without compensation
- ❖ Living in joint family setups with shared expenses
- ❖ Unspoken expectation to sacrifice your dreams "for the family"

These responsibilities are deeply rooted in Indian culture, but when they collide with couple goals like buying a house, saving for retirement, or building a business, conflict and confusion are inevitable.

Real-life case studies

Case Study 1: "My Parents, Your Burden?"

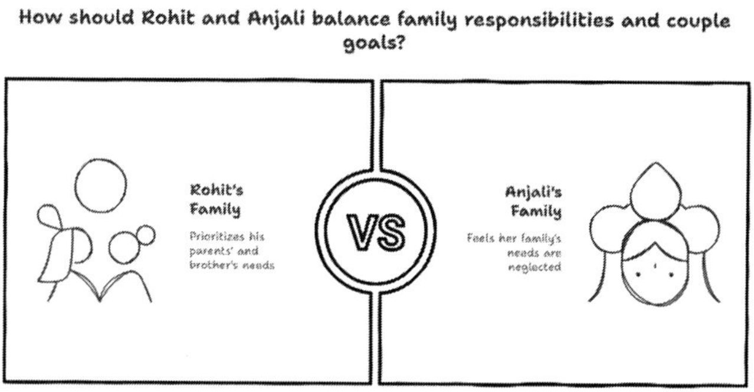

The Couple:

Rohit (32) and Anjali (29), newly married IT professionals in Bengaluru.

The Situation:

Rohit was sending ₹25,000/month to his retired parents and covering his younger brother's MBA fees (₹6 lakh). Anjali supported it initially but began to feel that her own family responsibilities were being sidelined, like saving for her father's knee surgery and contributing to her sister's wedding.

The Tension:

Their couple goals, saving for a down payment, planning a child, kept getting postponed. Fights grew frequent, often starting with budgets but ending in emotional statements like "You only care about your family."

I helped them put emotions aside and bring clarity through a joint family budget map:

- ❖ Fixed a "Family Support Budget" cap of ₹30,000/month, split as ₹18,000 for Rohit's parents and ₹12,000 for Anjali's family, reviewed annually.
- ❖ Created a "Couple Priority Fund": ₹20,000/month for house goals and ₹10,000 for emergencies.
- ❖ Used a simple Excel tracker with color codes: Green = Joint Priority,

Blue = Rohit's Family,

Pink = Anjali's Family.

Outcome:

Once it was all visible, Rohit saw the imbalance. They began planning their financial support consciously, with equal emotional weightage. Peace returned, and their trust deepened.

Study 2: "Big Fat Indian Wedding... On Our Savings"

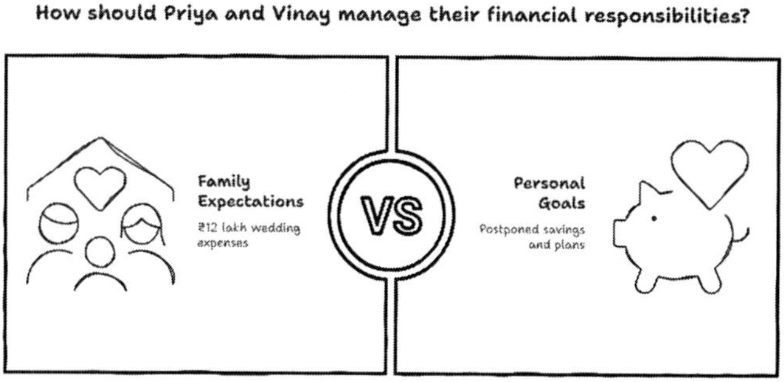

The Couple:

Priya (35) and Vinay (38), working professionals in Hyderabad, married for 10 years with two school-going kids.

The Situation:

Vinay's younger sister was getting married, and the family expected them to "take care of everything," catering, venue, gifts, decorations. The estimated cost? ₹12 lakh.

The Challenge:

Vinay felt emotionally obligated. Priya was furious, they had just begun a SIP for their kids' education and had no surplus funds.

My Intervention:

I brought both into a practical yet sensitive discussion:

- Drew up a wedding budget cap of ₹5 lakh, with ₹2 lakh as their direct contribution and ₹3 lakh as a "loan" to family, to be paid back over 2 years.
- I coached Vinay to communicate this respectfully to his parents, showing the long-term impact on their children's education and future.
- We also planned a gift registry and involved relatives in sharing the expenses, reducing the total burden.

Outcome:

The wedding was simpler but elegant. Vinay's family understood their limits. Priya felt heard, and they avoided dipping into their kids' funds.

Case Study 3: "I Want to Support My Mom, But He Thinks It's Optional"

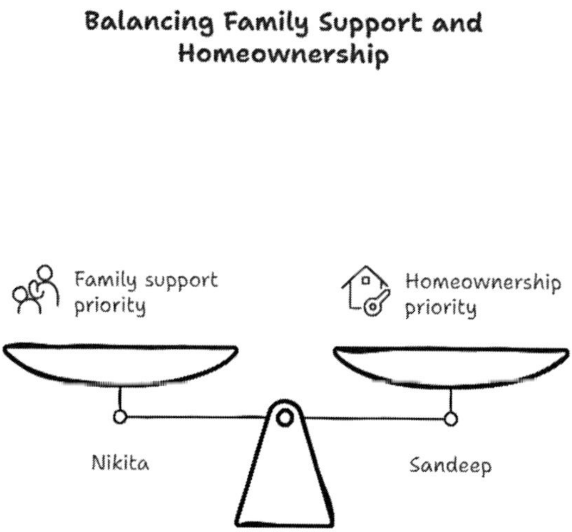

The Couple:

Nikita (31), HR Manager, and Sandeep (34), Project Manager, based in Pune. Married for 5 years. No kids yet.

The Situation:

Nikita lost her father during the pandemic. Her mother, a homemaker, was left with minimal savings and no pension. Nikita wanted to give her ₹15,000/month to cover rent and basic needs.

Sandeep wasn't against it, but felt it was a "temporary" thing, and began resisting whenever expenses went up. He believed most of their savings should go towards buying a flat.

The Emotional Tension:

Nikita started sending money secretly from her account. It led to emotional distance and frequent arguments:

"Why is helping my mother questioned while yours is considered a duty?"

My Financial Planning Intervention:

I sat down with both of them and introduced the concept of "Joint Family Budgeting with Emotional Equality."

The Plan:

❖ Created a Family Support Envelope: ₹25,000/month

- ₹ * ted a Family Support Env₹ * ted a Family Support Envelope: ₹25,000/monthes)

❖ Goal-Based Fund Split:

- ₹ * -Based Fund Split:home down payment
- ₹ * down payment for the couple's future

❖ Suggested term insurance and emergency fund for Nikita's mom so that unexpected hospital bills wouldn't derail their plans.

Outcome:

Sandeep understood the emotional weight of Nikita's responsibility. She felt respected. They started reviewing all family expenses together monthly. The house goal was delayed by a few months, but their emotional bond strengthened.

Case Study 4: "I Promised My Father I'd Fund My Sister's Education"

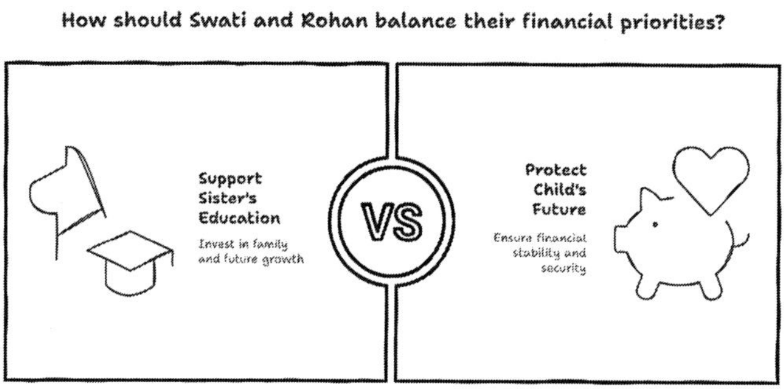

The Couple:

Swati (36), Architect, and Rohan (40), Bank VP, living in Delhi. Married for 12 years. One child, age 7.

The Situation:

Swati's younger sister got a full admission to an MBA college in Mumbai but needed ₹6 lakh in fees. Their father had retired and couldn't afford the amount. Swati wanted to sponsor it from their savings.

Rohan was supportive in principle but anxious. Their daughter's school fees, EMI, and investments were already stretched.

He feared dipping into fixed deposits meant for their child's future.

The Stress Point:

Swati started feeling guilty and resentful:

"If it were your brother, you'd just say yes. Why is my family a negotiation?"

My Role-

I acknowledged both emotions, Swati's promise and Rohan's fear. Then we created a phased plan to sponsor her sister without disrupting key financial goals.

The Plan:

❖ Loan + Support Combo:

- ₹2 lakh from savings
- ₹2 lakh as a soft loan from a relative (coordinated through Rohan's network)
- ₹2 lakh from an education loan in the sister's name (Swati as co-applicant)

❖ Savings Gap Refill Plan:

- ₹15,000/month SIP for 18 months to rebuild the withdrawn ₹2 lakh
- Set up a "backup emergency fund" using a short-term debt mutual fund

❖ Spoke to Swati's sister about taking up internships early to reduce dependency

Outcome:

Swati kept her word, and Rohan didn't feel financially cornered.

Most importantly, they made a joint decision with a future plan, not an impulsive sacrifice.

Financial Insight: Love without Losing Balance and what we learnt

When it comes to family obligations:

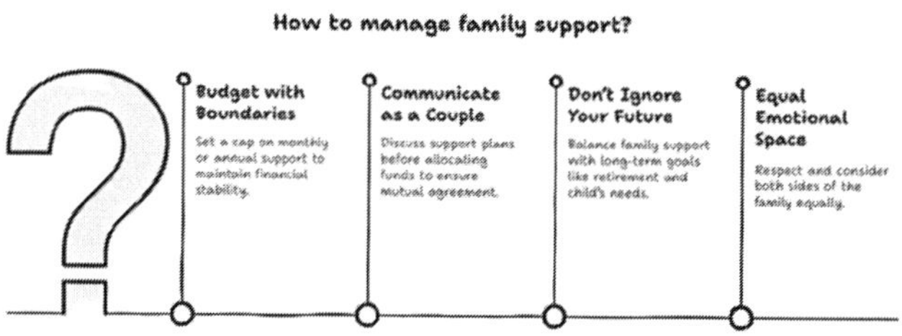

Couple's Checklist: Managing Family Pressure

1. [ ] Have we agreed on a monthly cap for family support?
2. [ ] Do we both feel heard when it comes to in-law expectations?
3. [ ] Are we balancing family duties with couple goals (home, child, travel)?
4. [ ] Have we built an emergency buffer to avoid last-minute stress?
5. [ ] Are we practicing empathy, not entitlement, with each other?

Wrapping it all up

In India, you're rarely married to just one person; you're married to a whole family. And that's beautiful, when it works.

But for it to work financially, couples must learn the delicate art of balancing tradition and boundaries. Giving to your family shouldn't mean taking from your future. With open conversations, joint planning, and mutual respect, you can honor both.

Because your wallet may hold more than two people, but your choices should always begin with you two.

Marriage in India extends beyond individuals.

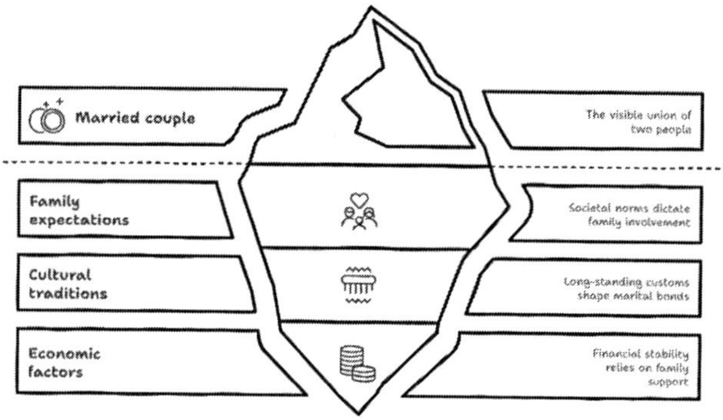

Chapter 10

Financial Burnout and Emotional Toll

How to stop money stress from becoming marriage stress.

We've talked about it all, joint accounts, secret debts, goal mismatches, in-laws, parenting expenses, and even the tough calls like insurance. But before we close this book, we must talk about one last, very real issue that quietly creeps in and shakes the foundation of even the strongest relationships:

Burnout. Emotional fatigue. And the toll money stress can take on love.

When Your Wallet Feels Empty, and So Do You

It's not always the big emergencies that drain us. Often, it's the slow, constant pressure:

- "Are we saving enough?"
- "Will we ever buy a house?"
- "I'm tired of living paycheck to paycheck."
- "I don't even want to open my bank app anymore."

Cycle of Financial Anxiety

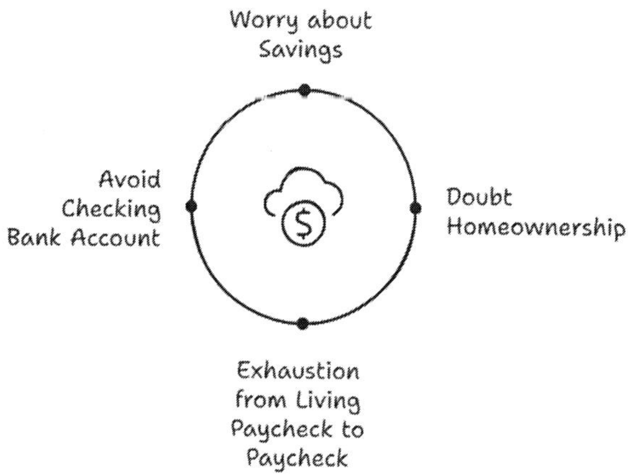

You might not even realize it, but one or both of you could be suffering from financial burnout, the emotional exhaustion that comes from constantly worrying about money, budgeting, paying bills, and trying to "do the right thing."

This stress doesn't stay in the spreadsheet.

It seeps into your dinner table conversations. Your sleep. Your intimacy.

One partner may shut down. The other may feel overwhelmed.

Resentment builds, not just about money, but about who is trying harder, who is worrying more, and who is not listening.

What Burnout Looks Like in a Couple

Let me give you two real-life patterns I see often:

1. The Over functionary vs. the Under functionary:
   One partner becomes hyper-involved, tracking every rupee, obsessing over goals, double-checking every spending. The other starts avoiding it altogether, shutting down or escaping into distractions. The more one chases control, the more the other pulls away.
2. The Silent Sufferers:
   Both partners feel anxious but pretend everything's fine. They smile, manage the bills, go to work, but deep down, they feel stuck and emotionally distant. It's like carrying invisible weights every single day.

How to Heal: Money May Be the Trigger, But Connection Is the Cure

Here's the truth:

Financial burnout isn't just a money problem.

It's a connection problem.

And the solution starts not with numbers, but with conversations and compassion.

Here's what helps:

1. Say It Out Loud
   Instead of silently coping, say what you feel:
   > "I feel overwhelmed managing everything."
   > "I miss when we used to talk about dreams, not just expenses."
   > "I'm scared we're falling behind."
   You don't need solutions right away. Start with the truth.
2. Take Breaks from Budgeting
   Yes, even money plans need off-days. Block a week where you don't talk about money at all.
   Instead, reconnect as partners. Watch a movie. Take a walk. Have fun without guilt.
3. Share the Load
   Don't let just one person carry all the financial responsibility. Divide tasks.
   Maybe one handles investments, the other reviews bills. Or maybe you sit together once a month and talk about everything, together.
4. Focus on Progress, Not Perfection

You don't have to follow every rule. You don't need to have it all figured out.

Even if you're just saving ₹500 this month or paying off one EMI, you're moving forward.

5. Get Help If Needed

   There is no shame in seeking support.

   Whether it's a financial advisor or a couples' therapist, sometimes talking to a neutral person makes all the difference.

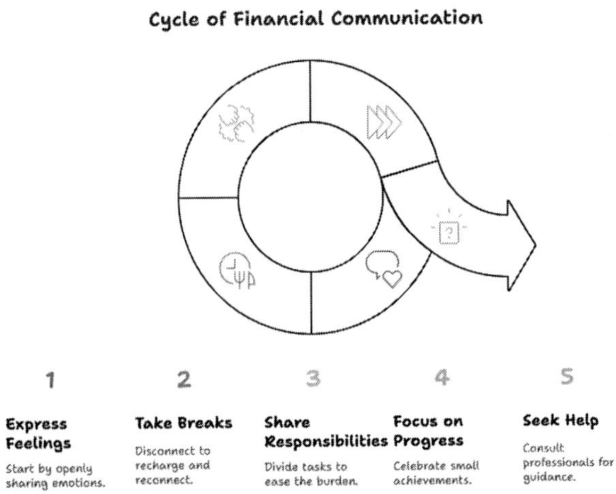

Let This Be a New Beginning

If you've made it to the end of this book, you've already taken a brave step that most couples don't.

You've chosen awareness over avoidance, teamwork over tension, and love over fear.

Financial stress is real, but so is financial healing.

You won't solve every problem overnight. But you can choose to face it together, with open eyes and open hearts.

This chapter isn't the end.

It's an invitation to live lighter, love deeper, and grow stronger together.

Money doesn't have to break you.

It can bond you—if you let it.

With gratitude,

Amar Khanna

Author | Finance coach

Helping couples talk money, without losing love.